THE BOOK OF SWINDLES

Selections from a Late Ming Collection

ZHANG YINGYU

Translated by Christopher Rea and Bruce Rusk

COLUMBIA UNIVERSITY PRESS   NEW YORK

Illuminating the Ming

This publication was made possible by a grant from the James P. Geiss Foundation, a private, non-profit operating foundation that sponsors research on China's Ming dynasty (1368–1644).

Columbia University Press wishes to express its appreciation for assistance given by the Pushkin Fund in the publication of this book.

Columbia University Press
Publishers Since 1893
New York   Chichester, West Sussex
cup.columbia.edu

Library of Congress Cataloging-in-Publication Data
Names: Zhang, Yingyu, active 16th century-17th century author. | Rea, Christopher G. translator. | Rusk, Bruce, 1972– translator.
Title: The book of swindles : selections from a late Ming collection / Zhang Yingyu ; translated by Christopher G. Rea and Bruce Rusk.
Description: New York : Columbia University Press, 2017. | Series: Translations from the Asian classics | Includes bibliographical references.
Identifiers: LCCN 2017000941 (print) | LCCN 2017021726 (ebook) | ISBN 9780231545648 (electronic) | ISBN 9780231178624 (cloth : alk. paper) | ISBN 9780231178631 (pbk.)
Subjects: LCSH: Swindlers and swindling—China—Anecdotes. | Fraud—China—Anecdotes.
Classification: LCC HV6699.C6 (ebook) | LCC HV6699.C6 Z43413 2017 (print) | DDC 364.16/3—dc23
LC record available at https://lccn.loc.gov/2017000941

Columbia University Press books are printed on permanent and durable acid-free paper.
Printed in the United States of America

Cover image: Courtesy of the National Museum of China. The cover illustration shows a detail from "Bustling Nanjing" (*Nandu fanhui tujuan* 南都繁繪圖卷), a long handscroll painting by an anonymous Ming dynasty artist (formerly attributed to Qiu Ying 仇英, 1494?–1552).

The Book of Swindles

TRANSLATIONS FROM THE ASIAN CLASSICS

Contents

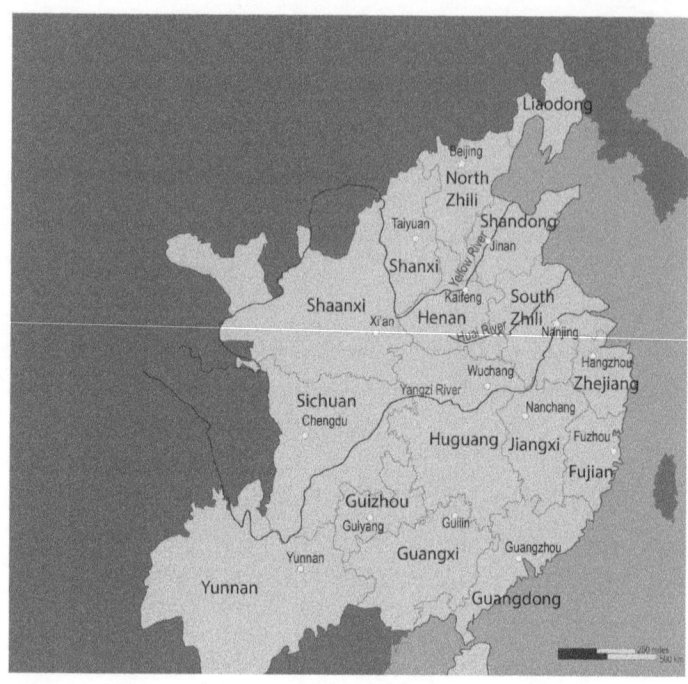

The Ming Empire in the Early Seventeenth Century

Southeastern China in the Early Seventeenth Century

Translators' Introduction

We live in an age of deception. Words and appearances mislead. Con artists prey on the unwary. The halls of power are choked with hypocrites, and the markets teem with frauds. Every stranger is a potential enemy, and one steps out the door at one's peril. In this world of swindlers, one must rely on one's wits to survive. How, then, to guard against the duplicity that seems to lurk behind every smiling face? Look to your kin, keep your possessions close, and trust no one.

But first, read this book.

The *Book of Swindles* is said to be the first Chinese story collection focused explicitly on the topic of fraud. It contains eighty-four stories classified into twenty-four types of swindle according to method, location, or perpetrator. A comment by the author, Zhang Yingyu (fl. 1612–17), follows nearly every story, and five additional stories appear within his commentary. Overall, the collection presents a panoramic survey of deceptive practices in contemporary society by a critic keenly interested in the dangers faced by common people, especially traveling merchants.

The crimes and cons recounted in the *Book of Swindles* take place mainly during the latter part of the Ming dynasty (1368–1644). During this period China underwent a flourishing of domestic and international commerce that created overnight fortunes. Zhang's collection captures a sense of the paranoia that resulted from the new risks and social change brought by this flow of money. Most of the stories concern stratagems for siphoning off some of the wealth circulating through the roads, canals, and market alleyways of the prosperous southern regions of the empire. Swindlers and marks hail from places as far north as Beijing, as far west as Sichuan, and as far south as Guangdong and Guangxi, but most of the action takes place in the region between the southern capital in Nanjing (Beijing, to the north, was the primary capital) and the southeastern coastal province of Fujian.

Zhang Yingyu refers to the agents of illicit appropriations of wealth as *gun*, which literally means "cudgel" but denoted anyone who made a living through crime. The methods of these "crooks," as we translate the term, could be violent, but in Zhang's stories always involve some element of deception and cunning.[1] He calls their stratagems "swindles" (*pian*) and focuses on the crooks' cleverness and creativity in manipulating victims.

The purpose of the book, according to its original title, is to protect the reader from such crimes. The woodblocks from which the first edition was printed, in or soon after 1617, label it *A New Book for Foiling Swindlers, Based on Worldly Experience* (*Jianghu lilan dupian xinshu*), and, to be sure, knowledge of crooks' techniques could help a reader defend against them. Yet the *Book* serves equally well as a manual for perpetrating swindles. And simply as a source of entertainment, it offers a wealth of narrative detail and describes crimes to which the average reader is unlikely to fall victim, such as eunuch cannibalism. Zhang Yingyu appends to the stories comments that vacillate between stern disapproval of the crooks' predations and connoisseurial appreciation of their ingenuity. Such equivocality permeates the book, both affirming and undermining the idea that human actions should be judged by a universal moral standard. Perhaps this is why modern editions have been entitled both *The Book Against Swindles* (*Fangpian jing*) and *The Book of Swindles* (*Pian jing*).

Our translation follows the latter title, which classifies the collection as a *jing*, or "classic."[2] In premodern China, this label was reserved for the core texts of a particular domain of knowledge: the philosophical classics of antiquity that served as the basis for orthodox Confucian learning; the religious scriptures of Buddhism and Daoism; and, later, the Bible. The term was eventually applied to less weighty fields: there were classics of tea, of chess, and of the boudoir.[3] The *Book of Swindles*, like these other works, has been recognized as a *jing* for offering a topical exposition that aims to be definitive, authoritative, and comprehensive.

In this introduction, we discuss a few ways to appreciate this landmark work in Chinese literary history, which offers words of warning for a world in peril.

The Swindle Story

Zhang Yingyu did not call his book a "classic," but he did treat the "crook's playbook," as he once refers to it, as worthy of familiarity and appreciation. Crooks, Zhang suggests, have their own shared body of specialized knowledge, and he treats ingenious scams as products of learning and skill. Crooks know what is to be gained, whom to target, where and how to lay a trap—and when to take the touch and scram. Most impressive to Zhang Yingyu are those swindles that reveal the perpetrator's deep understanding of the psychology of a particular group—miserly peasants, say, or civil service examination candidates—or of an individual. The swindler's nemesis is the "old hand," an experienced traveler (often a merchant) with a similar knowledge base who knows how to recognize scams and thwart them. A recursive theory of mind underlies this pair's ongoing battle of wits, in which each opponent might say to the other: I understand your understanding of me better than you understand it yourself.

The focus on ruses and ingenuity calls to mind other classics of strategic thinking such as the *Art of War* (whose author, Sun Zi, is mentioned in the book's 1617 preface by Xiong Zhenji) and the later *Thirty-Six Stratagems*, both of which exalt the use of deception in warfare.[4] Zhang Yingyu also mentions by name Zhuge Liang (181–234), the famed military strategist of the Three Kingdoms period. Successful ruses on the battlefield or in the halls of power, born of superior insight, self-possession, and desperation to survive, became the stuff of history. They changed the fates of armies, rulers, and kingdoms. The *Book of Swindles* concerns itself with similar principles and methods in the more mundane realms of commerce and civil society.[5] The effect of every individual scam is local. Only when taken in aggregate do these stories suggest an empire of endemic criminality.

American confidence artists of the early twentieth century distinguished between the short con—the momentary encounter in which the victim was taken for whatever he had on his person—and the big con, in which, over an extended period of time, the mark was persuaded to draw on additional resources.[6] This Ming dynasty "crooks' playbook" includes everything from simple street hustles to elaborate put-up jobs involving several actors and multiple stages. The takings range from nothing (in the case of foiled plots) to vast fortunes; some victims die at the hands of crooks. If the classic American confidence man saw his work as superior to that of the common thug and eschewed the use of force,[7] the *gun* employed violence as one tool among many.

The swindle story, in Zhang Yingyu's telling, is less a whodunit than a *how*dunit. We generally know from the outset who is the swindler and who the mark, and wait to see how the interaction plays out. The aesthetic is procedural: the storyteller holds us in suspense about how the ruse will unfold and whether it will succeed. Chance plays a role—Zhang's commentaries sometimes attribute a result to the workings of fate—but human ingenuity and experience are the main drivers of narrative cause and effect.

This is one similarity that Zhang's swindle stories share with court case fiction, an established genre by the late Ming, which anatomizes the investigation and prosecution of a crime.[8] At the center of these stories is the magistrate, whose wisdom and perspicuity enable him to crack the case. His investigative and deductive prowess derives from his understanding both of social institutions and of the criminal mind, and he can manipulate dissemblers into confessing or unwittingly revealing the truth. Zhang Yingyu's work shares with this genre an appreciation of ingenuity, but finds this quality on both sides of the law. Principals in the *Book of Swindles* often bring their disputes to the local magistrate, who reveals new information about the swindle in the process of reconstructing the case. Yet, unlike standard court case narratives, many of Zhang's stories shows representatives of the law in an unflattering light, notably the famously wise and incorruptible Judge Bao, whose one appearance in the collection is as a dupe ("An Officer Reprimands a Captured Criminal in Order to Halve His Flogging").

The *Book of Swindles* overlaps with a variety of other genres, including tales of retribution, supernatural tales, classical tales (*chuanqi*), jokes, and anecdotes. Zhang draws on stock scenarios and character types from vernacular fiction and drama, such as the charlatan Daoist, the duplicitous broker, and the foolish scion of a rich family. In this, his stories are very much of their time. We find dropped bags, ingenious thievery, and imposture in fiction by contemporaries such as Feng Menglong (1574–1645), Ling Mengchu (1580–1644), and Li Yu (1610–80). Venal monks and eunuchs, lying procuresses and go-betweens appear in a wide array of vernacular literature, including contemporary novels such as *The Water Margin* (*Shui hu zhuan*, first extant imprint 1589) and *Plum in the Golden Vase* (*Jin ping mei*, first extant imprint 1610). "A Buddhist Nun Scatters Prayer Beads to Lure a Woman Into Adultery," for example, concerns a rich man who employs an old woman to help him seduce the wife of a man away on business. The progression of the seduction in Zhang's story parallels that in "The Pearl Vest" and the more famous story it inspired, "The Pearl-Sewn Shirt," which appears in Feng Menglong's *Stories Old and New* (1620). All three stories also share specific details such as the successful attempt by the old woman (a nun, in Zhang's story) to incite the wife's lust by discussing her own amorous past, and the streetside display of pearls or beads to attract the wife's attention.[9]

Many cultures possess a rich body of lore about tricksters who upend the social order, swindlers who exploit its loopholes, and thieves who sever the bonds between people and property. Such stories not only reflect social realities, they also create tropes that shape how people imagine the world they live in. The idea of the confidence man, for example, loomed large in the bustling cities and burgeoning frontiers of the antebellum United States. From the roads, rails, and riverboats, he soon became a fixture in penny papers, city guides, and novels, ever ready to prey on the disoriented inhabitants of a world of strangers.[10] Zhang Yingyu's tales of swindlers likewise reflect the anxieties and preoccupations of his time and place. His impulses to compile, classify, and anatomize cases of deception, however, are not unique. The growth in population, mass printing, and urbanization propelled by the Industrial Revolution also gave rise to commoditized versions of the cautionary tale. Around the turn of the nineteenth century, for example, travelers to London might pick up a copy of Richard King, Esq.'s short volume *The New Cheats of London Exposed; or the frauds and tricks of the town laid open to both sexes, being a guard against the iniquitous practices of that Metropolis* (ca. 1792). Herman Melville's *The Confidence-Man: His Masquerade* (1857) depicts the methods of a serial scammer who adopts a variety of personæ in his efforts to separate riverboat passengers from their money. The quintessential nineteenth-century entertainer P. T. Barnum, a savvy exploiter of popular interest in debunking "experts," cast a wide net with his best-selling anthology *The Humbugs of the World: An Account of Humbugs, Delusions, Impositions, Quackeries, Deceits and Deceivers, Generally, in All Ages* (1866). Closer to Zhang Yingyu's age, *Don Quixote* (Part One, 1605), Francisco de Quevedo's *The Swindler* (1626), and other Spanish picaresque novels popularized the literary archetypes of the itinerant rogue, the juvenile trickster, and the delusive wanderer.[11] Fraud and deception are endemic to humanity, yet stories about ingenuity and cunning appear, like their shape-shifting protagonists, in remarkable variations.

Traversing River and Lake

Many of the encounters in the *Book of Swindles* involve a particular and highly charged social scenario: travel among strangers.[12] Porters carry examination candidates only half the promised route and then stop to extort a higher fare. Women seduce merchants far from home, prostitute female relatives, frame innocent men, steal horses on the highway, and enter into sham marriages for purposes of murder and extortion. Waggish literati on pleasure trips seek out and outwit courtesans and officials. Crooks traveling by land and water impersonate rich scions, Daoists, alchemists, and acquaintances of powerful officials in order to fleece merchants and examination hopefuls. Buddhist monks and nuns, Daoist priests, and court eunuchs are especially notorious in Zhang's work as lechers, procuresses, bogus alchemists, and murderous sorcerers. While some swindles involve family members and hometown acquaintances, most occur away from home or involve a visiting outsider.

Like much Chinese fiction, the tales in the *Book of Swindles* are presented as history, yet Zhang Yingyu's interest is not historiographic or biographical. Only one story's title mentions a real person by name ("Chen Quan Scams His Way Into the Arms of a Famous Courtesan"), but this protagonist was by no means a famous figure, so it seems likely that celebrity was not the draw.[13] Other stories feature much better-known historical personages, yet their titles only describe the action; in other words, Zhang presents them as generic examples of recurring phenomena. Stories based on real events, or that mention specific dates, place names, and historical personages, are to some degree fictionalized. (Even some of the place names in stories cannot be identified with any known locale and are likely fictive.) Zhang Yingyu's focus is on interactions among ordinary folk, including those at the lowest levels of the social order (peasants, street cleaners, itinerant peddlers). Their names hardly matter; what matters is their skill in moving through a hostile environment of untrustworthy strangers.

The "worldly experience" that Zhang shares is derived from the imaginary realm of the *jianghu*, a term appearing in the collection's full title. The Rivers and Lakes, as *jianghu* might be translated literally, is a transitory space of indeterminate geography and fluid identities, a social milieu bounded on one extreme by the order of the state and on the other by the wilds beyond civilization. It is a place of refuge for political exiles, outlaws, martial artists, socially marginal figures, and people hiding from the law. It is also a realm of commerce plied by merchants, petty entrepreneurs, civil service examinations candidates, officials heading to and from their posts, monks, medicine men, soothsayers, entertainers, mendicants, and swindlers. In literature, drama, and popular culture, the human geography of the *jianghu* is defined less by individuals than by types of roughly predictable appearance and behavior. But the overarching maxim of the *jianghu* is that people are often not what they seem.

Vulnerability increases with distance from home—as does the lure of profit. In the very first story of the collection, a horse trader from the inland province of Jiangxi travels over a thousand miles to Nanjing, only to encounter a swindler there and be dragged to court for serving as his unwitting accomplice. In the "Showing Off Wealth" section, a merchant from Shandong province covers a similar distance on a cloth-buying trip to Fujian, during which he is unknowingly pursued by a swindler in disguise. While passing through Jiangxi province, the crook dupes the local magistrate, who hails from Guangdong province to the south, into believing that he is the son of a powerful Surveillance Intendant serving in Fujian. The magistrate's courteous reception convinces the merchant to trust the imposter, who leaves him drunk and broke before he reaches his destination. Experienced swindlers know that it's easier to hook a fish—or, in this case, two—out of water.

The Author and His Voice

Zhang Yingyu is an obscure figure. The *Book of Swindles* is the only known work to appear under his name, and no record of him survives in any biographical source.[14] Zhang lived during the Wanli period (1563–1620) of the Ming dynasty; according to the 1617 preface, he hailed from Jianyang county in Fujian. This seems probable, given that the first extant version of the book was printed there; that over half of the stories with identifiable locales take place in Fujian; and that terms from Fujian dialect occur in many stories.[15] This biographical information is contradicted within the *Book of Swindles* itself, however: chapter headings in the Ming edition identify Zhang as being from Zhejiang province (just north of Fujian); one possibility is that his family was originally from Zhejiang but he lived in Fujian.[16]

Zhang's commentaries are one of the outstanding features of the *Book of Swindles*. Commentary, including that by the author of the main text (autocommentary), is common in many genres of premodern Chinese literature, including Ming vernacular fiction. Early historians pioneered this practice, appending statements to their biographies and topical essays in which they spoke in their own voice and expressed judgments about the narrative presented in the main text. Later authors, editors, and critics were often eager to clarify plot points or gloss expressions to make sure that the moral of the story did not escape the reader.[17] In commenting on his own stories, Zhang Yingyu performs several roles. He speaks as a moralist, apportioning blame for the swindle. Sometimes he attributes this to the folly or naïveté of the victim rather than to the venality of the crook—the dupe should have known better and avoided a bad situation. He speaks as an expert on cons and crimes, judging the deceptive technique of the swindler, the precautions or retaliation of the mark, the actions of people who intervene in the proceedings, and the perspicuity of the official trying the case. He also speaks as a witness, corroborating, contradicting, or supplying facts based on supposed firsthand knowledge; examples include the stories "Forged Letters from the Education Intendant Report Auspicious Dreams," "Marrying a Street Cleaner and Provoking His Death," and "A Geomancer Uses His Wife to Steal a Good Seed." In virtually every instance, he not only comments on the individual case but also extrapolates a general moral lesson or a piece of practical advice. And in some cases the commentary contains additional material, even entire stories.[18]

To understand most of the stories in the *Book of Swindles*, a Ming reader would have needed only literacy in simple literary Chinese and familiarity with basic social institutions, the type of knowledge one might expect of an educated merchant. Zhang's commentaries, however, often use more formal language and make historical and literary allusions that only a reader with more classical training would recognize. One recurring point of reference is the *Book of Changes* (*Yijing* or *I Ching*), the ancient divination manual that became a Confucian classic. It seems likely that Zhang was a student of the *Changes*, perhaps in preparation for the civil service examinations. (Xiong Zhenji mentions the *Changes* in his preface as a model for the *Book of Swindles* itself.) Some of these allusions are unmarked and presume familiarity with the text. The *Book of Changes* is arranged around a set of sixty-four figures called "hexagrams," each consisting of a stack of six horizontal lines. In divination, a process of manipulating reeds or tossing coins would yield a hexagram and a focus on particular lines within it. The text of the *Changes* consists of short, cryptic statements for each hexagram and for each line, as well as several layers of additional commentary. A diviner would come to the *Changes* with a situation in mind and interpret it using the texts and lines that the divination process yielded. Zhang Yingyu also uses the *Changes* as a general repository of wisdom and insight, invoking its words for guidance on all sorts of ethical and practical decisions. For example, in his comment on the story "Bringing Mirrors Aboard a Boat Invites a Nefarious Plot," in which a loyal servant protects his spendthrift master who turns a business trip into a sightseeing jaunt, he alludes to portions of the description of the fifty-sixth hexagram, Lü 旅 (Traveling), that mention the importance of a good serving boy. Since the *Book of Changes* is not mentioned by title, Zhang either assumed that his reader would catch the unmarked reference or was unconcerned about readers who would not.

Late Ming Society

Most of the stories in the *Book of Swindles* are set in the context in which they were written, the society of the late Ming (roughly

1550–1644), and in particular the highly commercialized regions of the southeast. The book was first printed in Jianyang, a major center of private publishing in Fujian province, and its author, as mentioned earlier, hailed from either there or Zhejiang to the immediate north. Both regions figure prominently in the stories as setting or as characters' place of origin. These places and some of the surrounding areas underwent profound social and economic change from the middle of the sixteenth century onward. Commerce became more and more central to the lives of ordinary people and was increasingly conducted with silver rather than through barter. Complex regional, interregional, and international trade networks moved goods and people over long distances. In the southeast this was facilitated by efficient boat travel via rivers, lakes, and canals. Specialized intermediaries stepped in to establish trust; they appear in the stories as brokers (who mediate transactions and hold payments in escrow), wholesalers, innkeepers, and local agents who act on behalf of a visiting merchant. Profits from trade concentrated wealth in the hands of merchants and others not tied to older power structures such as landowning and office holding. Commerce shook up the social order by enabling new groups to acquire literacy, to purchase luxury goods and the trappings of culture, and to prepare for the civil service examinations.[19]

The Ming had no hereditary aristocracy, aside from the large but mostly powerless extended imperial lineage. Families with a tradition of examination success and office holding, however, often viewed themselves as leaders of local society. Many members of this traditional elite saw the forces of commerce as eroding the proper social order. The boom in commercial publishing, meanwhile, spurred changes in popular culture. Thanks to the enormous output of publishers, printers, book sellers, authors, and editors, the vernacular culture of the late Ming is far more accessible to us than that of any earlier period in Chinese history. The era saw the proliferation of works of literature, reference books, and religious texts accessible to, intended for, and in many cases produced by nonelites.[20]

The *Book of Swindles*, a book primarily for and about merchants, is one such work. Traveling merchants are the main characters of most of Zhang's stories. In stories involving merchants interacting with brokers, innkeepers, money changers, officials, farmers, clerks, prostitutes, or members of other professions, Zhang speaks for the merchant. "Impersonating the Son of an Official to Steal a Merchant's Silver," for example, shows the risks merchants face in dealing with officialdom: a cloth merchant comes to grief when he tries to fulfill a social obligation to a traveling companion who appears to be the son of a powerful official. "A Eunuch Cooks Boys to Make a Tonic of Male Essence" begins with a screed arguing that when taxes impede commerce they harm not just merchants but society as a whole. In "Stealing a Business Partner's Riches Only to Lose One's Own," a traveler swindles a fellow merchant from the same hometown, prompting Zhang Yingyu to lament the exploitation of a lonely traveler's desire for kinship. Many of his appended comments address readers directly as merchants, or assume that commerce is their profession.

Officialdom

Many of the stories involve state institutions, especially the criminal justice system and the civil service examinations. The Ming empire was governed through a multitiered set of institutions, staffed by centrally appointed officials, and governed by written laws and regulations. Central government offices were located in the capital, Beijing, with smaller shadow versions based in the secondary southern capital, Nanjing. Most of the rest of the empire was divided up into nested administrative units: provinces, divided into prefectures, subdivided into counties. In charge of each unit was at least one centrally appointed official who worked with a staff of local subordinates in an office complex called the *yamen*. The smallest administrative unit, the county, could be quite large: over the course of the Ming dynasty, the number of counties remained roughly constant at about 1,400, while the population of a county grew to an average of over 160,000 and a maximum of perhaps one million at the time when these stories were written. The county magistrate was in charge of almost all civilian administrative matters in his jurisdiction: tax collection, public works, criminal and civil law, and the performance of state religious rituals. A prefect would oversee the same matters for the several counties within his prefecture.

Most ordinary people, consequently, had little or no contact with their local magistrate. Given the opacity of the justice system and its reliance on torture to extract confessions from witnesses as well as suspects, many preferred to keep it that way. Zhang Yingyu calls the *yamen* a "thicket of swindles" and advises readers to avoid it at all costs. In his stories we occasionally catch glimpses of officials, but we encounter more of the people who did the day-to-day work of government: clerks, runners, constables, gatekeepers, and other underlings. The staff of a *yamen*, who were generally hired locally, were of vital importance because they acted as an interface between the populace and the state. Magistrates and prefects, who were typically appointed for terms of just three years and forbidden from serving in their home area, depended on them for local knowledge and to carry out their decisions.

Civil Service Examinations

Officials were selected by a system of performance reviews and recommendations, after having been recruited through an empire-wide system of examinations. The civil service examinations were open to most men (and even precocious boys), though in practice only those with the means to devote years to formal education took them. Even those not directly involved in the system were likely aware of it, if they had a smattering of education. Many exam takers were from merchant families and would return to commerce in the likely event that they failed to progress beyond the lowest levels of the system. Each examination lasted multiple days and involved a series of tests, each requiring a piece of writing on a topic chosen by the examiners and in a rigid, often formulaic format. Knowledge of Confucian classics and their commentaries, ancient and recent history, the forms of bureaucratic documents, and the major policy issues of the day were essential for examination success. Controls to prevent fraud in this high-stakes system, though far from foolproof, were strict. Examinees were sealed within a complex of individual carrels, and examiners, who set the topics, were brought in from outside the jurisdiction to reduce opportunities for corruption. Responses were anonymized by assigning each exam taker a code number, and scribes recopied written responses to avoid the recognition of individuals' handwriting. The examiners assessed them and then posted a ranked list of those who had passed. Those left off the list had failed. This process was repeated regularly in every county of the empire, and each exam was taken by thousands of men.

Those who passed local examinations (held at the county and/or prefectural level) were known informally as *xiucai*, or "distinguished talents." This status brought certain privileges, such as exemption from state labor service and protection from corporal punishment, but it generally did not qualify the holder for government office. *Xiucai* could go on to take an examination held triennially in each provincial capital, and those who passed (again, a minority) became a *juren* or "recommended man." *Juren* were eligible to hold office, but by the late Ming their numbers were so great that most received no appointment at all or only a low-ranking post, typically that of county magistrate or below. They could, however, proceed to the highest level of examinations, held every three years in Beijing. Success there made one a *jinshi* ("presented scholar"), from whose ranks the upper bureaucracy was drawn. In the *Book of Swindles*, officials at or above the rank of magistrate can be presumed to be *juren* or *jinshi*. *Xiucai* occasionally assist in swindles but feature more often as the targets of scammers promising a way to bribe the examiner.

Examination success and office holding alike brought to an individual and their family social prestige, legal protections, and the possibility of material gains. While official salaries were fairly low, the potential for income through customary payments (made ostensibly to offset expenses like legal fees) and outright corruption was enormous. Families were eager to ensure examination success for their offspring, and therefore vulnerable to predators. "Forged Letters from the Education Intendant Report Auspicious Dreams," based on events that allegedly took place in the year 1600, dramatizes a type of "good news scam" targeting such families that historical sources attest was being perpetrated as late as the eighteenth century.[21] Examination-related corruption (especially involving bribery or efforts to recruit political and intellectual allies) was a constant issue, despite extensive countermeasures. The *Book of Swindles* devotes an entire section of stories to "Corruption in Education," all concerning perversions of the examination process.

The Silver Standard

Money is the target of most crooks' schemes in the *Book of Swindles*. In the late Ming, it took two main forms: silver, which circulated unminted as ingots or lumps, and copper coins. (Paper money, which had been used earlier in the dynasty, became so deeply devalued by the mid-fifteenth century that it went out of circulation.) Loose copper coins served for small, everyday purchases, and strings of up to a thousand (attached through holes in the center) for larger expenditures. Silver, because of its greater density, was preferable for major transactions or long-distance transport. Private silversmiths cast ingots of various shapes—the most common being a pinch-waisted oval with flat sides and raised flanges around the top—and varying degrees of purity. For a minor transaction, one might use a fragment of a gram or less, sometimes snipped off of a larger ingot. In the *Book of Swindles*, all but the smallest transactions are carried out in silver. Although gold was also valuable in the Ming, it never served as money, only as a precious material for making jewelry and other luxury items. Such items, of both gold and silver, could be melted down and sold off, so both metals were useful as stores of value. By the late sixteenth century, silver was mainly used as a medium of exchange and served as the principal money of account: it was how many prices were denominated and how most taxes and larger private payments were collected. After two parties settled on a price, they had to weigh out the appropriate quantity, taking into account the proportion of silver in the alloy, which could vary from under 70 to nearly 100 percent.

Since silver was so ubiquitous and so variable, counterfeits were an ever-present risk. Several stories (most obviously in the section "Fake Silver," but also "Sticking a Plaster in the Eyes to Steal a Silver Ingot" in the section "Violence") allude to the problem. The purity of a piece of silver was assayed mainly through visual inspection, though a suspicious-looking ingot that might contain copper or lead could be pried open with a chisel. Other stories, in the section "Alchemy," describe the allure of using magic to produce silver (not gold) from base metals or even from thin air. Zhang Yingyu seems to accept that some of these supernatural ways of making money are real, even as he alleges that many of the "alchemists" one might encounter are frauds.

Large transactions might involve a process of "sealing" and escrow. After silver of the agreed-upon quantity and purity was weighed out it was placed, in sight of both parties, in a crate, case, or other container that would be closed up and covered with paper strips to which both parties affixed the impressions of their respective stamps (seals made of wood, stone, or metal). Opening or otherwise tampering with such a package would damage the seal, so an unbroken seal would assure the seller that the desired funds were available and intact, and the buyer could hold on to the payment until the deal was finalized.

Sealed packages of silver feature prominently in stories about bribes to officials and government clerks: the bribe-taking party would want to be sure in advance that the funds were available, just as the briber would want to make sure that the desired outcome had been achieved before handing over the silver. The complexity of this process is evident in stories about corruption in the civil service examinations. For example, "Affixing Seals in a Functionary's Chambers," in which an official is bribed to ensure a candidate's success on the exams, describes both parties' close attention to the container used as well as the location and timing of the sealing process. When the integrity of the process is violated, as in the next story, "Silver with Sham Seals Is Switched for Bricks," it can seem like magic.

Silver was measured in a unit of weight called *liang*, which we translate as "ounce." It measured approximately 37 grams, though the precise weight varied by region and context. (Government weights were slightly different from those used in the marketplace.) This unit is also known in English by the Malay word *tael*, which was used for centuries in international trade in East and Southeast Asia. The *liang* was further divided into tenths (*qian*, traditionally translated as "mace") and hundredths (*fen*, traditionally "canadareen"); for consistency, we have converted all these references to fractions of an ounce. Ounces were the measure for other goods as well, including gold; heavier commodities such as food were usually weighed in *jin* of sixteen ounces, which we translate as "pound." The other important unit in this collection, which we leave untranslated, is the geographic measure of distance *li*, which is about 500 meters or a third of a mile.

Sources and Influence

The variation in content and style among the stories makes it clear that Zhang Yingyu drew inspiration from sources beyond his personal experience and imagination. These include literary works in the genres mentioned above, biographies of historical personages, philosophical classics, folklore, and local gossip or hearsay. For example, "Swindling the Salt Commissioner While Disguised as Daoists" adapts with little modification two anecdotes from biographical sources about the poet Tang Yin (1470–1524). In other cases, it appears that the stories are copied from another work that we have not been able to identify. Some stories close with an explicit moral, after which Zhang's comment provides an additional moral. In the case of "Flashy Clothing Incites Larceny," for example, Zhang draws a lesson that contradicts the internal moral, suggesting that he had copied the narrative wholesale from another source.[22] The six stories in the section "Corruption in Education" all end with the formulaic phrase "This is a warning against. . . ." This pattern appears nowhere else in the collection, suggesting that this cycle derived from a single source. Although Zhang Yingyu generally does not identify his sources, in the commentary on a story about Fake Silver (not translated here), he describes finding a pamphlet describing techniques for distinguishing grades of silver, then copies out the entire text. The account of monkey boy Xie, the third story nested in the commentary on "A Geomancer Uses His Wife to Steal a Good Seed," was, Zhang says, related to him by a geomancer in Xie's home county. Stylistic and intertextual evidence alike suggest that this is more an edited and rewritten anthology than a single-authored collection of stories.

Just as Zhang's stories often involve travel, the stories themselves traveled across space and time. Versions of some of them, or similar plot elements, appear in other works, but it is impossible to be certain of the original source.[23] For example, a version of the salt-lick trick from "A Buddhist Monk Identifies a Cow as His Mother" turns up, over a century later, in chapter 24 of the great Qing novel *The Scholars* (*Rulin waishi*, 1750)—possibly drawn from the *Book of Swindles*, but possibly from elsewhere; another version appears in the 1808 travelogue *The Moon Through the Cloud Rift on a Rainy Night* by the late Edo period writer Kyokutei Bakin (1767–1848), a known aficionado of the *Book of Swindles*.[24]

Despite abundant interest in the subject matter, there were no reprintings of the book in China in the first three centuries after its initial appearance. In Japan, however, it seems to have been more popular and was widely disseminated. An edition in Chinese with Japanese annotations appeared in Kyoto in 1770, followed by further editions in the nineteenth century, including a Japanese translation in 1879 and more recent academic studies.[25] In China, while swindles and deception remained popular as subject matter of literature and drama, after the 1600s no new edition was printed, to our knowledge, until the late 1980s or early 1990s, when reproductions of a Ming woodblock copy appeared in a series of imprints aimed at a scholarly audience.[26] These were soon followed by more accessible typeset editions in various parts of China (Tianjin, 1992; Beijing, 1993; Guangzhou, 1993; Zhengzhou, 1994; Shenyang, 1994; Shijiazhuang, 1995).[27] A 1997 edition pairing the original text with translation into vernacular Chinese made the work even more approachable for contemporary readers, though the editor cut passages he found obscene or vulgar.[28] There has been little scholarship on the *Book of Swindles* in Western languages, mainly two introductory but useful articles.[29]

Despite the longtime obscurity of Zhang Yingyu's work, modern China has seen several surges of interest in swindle stories more broadly. Collections of swindle stories proliferated during the late Qing and Republican eras (ca. 1890s–1949), a period of political turmoil, abortive modernization efforts, and rapid urbanization.[30] Swindle stories came into vogue again during the Reform and Opening period that followed Mao Zedong's death in 1976, and their popularity has if anything intensified since then. In addition to the new editions of Zhang Yingyu's work, since the 1990s at least half a dozen swindle story collections have appeared in China, including some comparing swindles old and new or appending commentaries. Social trust, or lack thereof, continues to be an issue of keen popular concern.

About This Translation

This translation presents forty-four titled stories, representing just over half of Zhang Yingyu's collection. We have included at least one story from each of the twenty-four sections, and all of the stories in the sections "The Bag Drop," "Brokers," "Showing Off Wealth," "Poetry," "Corruption in Education," and "Pandering." Our sample aims to illustrate the variety of Zhang's collection; to highlight recurring themes such as silver, imposture, and Zhang Yingyu's moral touchstone of the *Book of Changes*; and to include some notable outliers in terms of content or style. The last include "Eating Human Fetuses to Fake Fasting," a gruesome tale of cannibalism with an appended "bonus story" about a true immortal who could live without food; "Marrying a Street Cleaner and Provoking His Death," which stands out for its elaborate use of wordplay to convey an implicit moral; and "Silver with Sham Seals Is Switched for Bricks," in which our editor—for once at a loss admits that the swindler's technique remains a mystery even to him.

We have based our translation on the digitized version of a Ming woodblock copy, issued by the Cunren tang of Jianyang, Fujian, and held at the Tōyō Bunka Kenkyūjo (Institute for Advanced Studies on Asia) of the University of Tokyo. It includes an illustration at the head of each of the four *juan*, and several missing pages have been replaced with handwritten supplements. We compared this with a copy of the same edition held at the Harvard-Yenching Library and also available in digitized form; this copy is missing the third and final story in Type 7 ("Enticement to Gambling"), "A Gambling Addict Falls Prey to an Ingenious Trick." We have also consulted a manuscript held in the National Archives of Japan, which is the source of the 1617 Xiong Zhenji preface.[31] It appears to have been copied from the earliest woodblock edition, issued by the Juren tang of Yu Yingke, a member of the most prominent lineage of Jianyang publishers.[32] No original copies of this imprint are known, but it is likely that the Harvard and University of Tokyo copies of the Cunren tang edition were printed from the same set of woodblocks, modified to change the name of the publisher and to remove the preface.[33]

The abundance of minor errors such as incorrect characters and internal discrepancies (including variations in formatting and inconsistencies between story titles in the main text and the table of contents) suggest that the book was produced with lax editorial oversight.[34] We also consulted two modern editions: *Pian jing* (The Classic of Swindles), published by Jiangxi shifan daxue chubanshe in 2008; and *Fangpian jing* (The Classic of Foiling Swindles), an expurgated edition with vernacular Chinese translation and commentaries by Ding Xiaoshan, published by Zhongguo wenlian chubanshe in 1997, and the selected modern Japanese translation by Itō et al.

Acknowledgments

We are grateful to Professor Robert Hegel, Professor Sarah Schneewind, and two anonymous reviewers at Columbia University Press for their comments on the manuscript, as well as to our editors, Jennifer Crewe and Leslie Kriesel. We also received valuable assistance and feedback from fellow panelists and audience members at the Association for Asian Studies annual meeting in Seattle in 2014; from Rusk's students, who were guinea pigs for some early draft translations; and from TJ Hinrichs, Patricia Rea, Ding Xiang Warner, and library staff at UBC, Harvard, and Cornell.

Notes

1. The book uses *gun* 棍 ("cudgel" or "staff") and *guanggun* 光棍 ("bright [or bare] cudgel") interchangeably, and we use "crook" for both. On this class of people in the Ming urban environment and related terms for them, see Han Dacheng 韓大成, *Mingdai chengshi yanjiu* 明代城市研究 (Beijing: Zhongguo renmin daxue chubanshe, 1991), 341–58.

2. In the title we render *jing* as "Book," following established translations for classics such as *Book of Documents* (*Shujing* 書經), *Book of Poems* (*Shijing* 詩經), and *Book of Changes* (*Yijing* 易經).

3. For a detailed analysis of the *Classic of Whoring* (*Piaojing* 嫖經), see Yuming He, *Home and the World: Editing the "Glorious Ming" in Woodblock-Printed Books of the Sixteenth and Seventeenth Centuries* (Cambridge, MA: Harvard University Asia Center, 2013), appendix 2.

4. The *Art of War* (*Sunzi bingfa* 孫子兵法) dates to ca. 500–450 B.C.E. The *Thirty-Six Stratagems* (*Sanshiliu ji* 三十六計) is a terse list of strategies based on historical examples; in its present form it may have come together only in the mid-twentieth century.

5. Only one story describes a scam with empirewide repercussions. In "Magic Reflections in Water Incite a Rebellion" ("Fashui zhaoxing sou moufan" 法水照形唆謀反), not translated here, a Buddhist monk puts a charm on a basin of water that reflects visions of grandeur to the beholder, leading one official to attempt an (unsuccessful) rebellion.

6. David Maurer, *The Big Con: The Story of the Confidence Man* (New York: Anchor, 1999 [1940]), 1–4.

7. Ibid., 168–72.

8. On the *Book of Swindles'* links to the court case (*gong'an* 公案) genre, see Daniel M. Youd, "Beyond *Bao*: Moral Ambiguity and the Law in Late Imperial Chinese Narrative Literature," in *Writing and Law in Late Imperial China: Crime, Conflict, and Judgment*, ed. Robert E. Hegel and Katherine Carlitz (Seattle: University of Washington Press, 2007), 215–33. One famous collection published during Zhang Yingyu's lifetime is the *Hundred Cases of Judge Bao* (*Bao Longtu pan baijia gong'an* 包龍圖判百家公案, 1594).

9. "The Pearl-Sewn Shirt" is available in multiple translations, including in Feng Menglong, *Stories Old and New: A Ming Dynasty Collection*, trans.

Shuhui Yang and Yunqin Yang (Seattle: University of Washington Press, 2011), 9–47. A translation and discussion of "The Pearl Vest" appears in Patrick Hanan, "The Making of *The Pearl-Sewn Shirt* and *The Courtesan's Jewel Box*," *Harvard Journal of Asiatic Studies* 33, no. 3–4 (1973): 124–53.

10. For a useful introduction to the confidence man as a trope in American literature, see William E. Lenz, *Fast Talk and Flush Times: The Confidence Man as a Literary Convention* (Columbia, MO: University of Missouri Press, 1985).

11. See Michael Alpert, trans., *Lazarillo de Tormes and The Swindler: Two Spanish Picaresque Novels*, rev. ed. (New York: Penguin, 2003).

12. On travel through empire and the resulting extreme ethical situations involving seeming strangers who turn out to be kin, in Ming-Qing literature and drama, see Tina Lu, *Accidental Incest, Filial Cannibalism, and Other Peculiar Encounters in Late Imperial Chinese Literature* (Cambridge, MA: Harvard University Asia Center, 2008).

13. Chen Quan is mentioned as a lower degree holder (*xiucai*) and writer of humorous verse in Zhou Hui's 周暉 (fl. 1610) *Nanjing Miscellany*. Zhou, *Jinling suoshi* 金陵瑣事 (Beijing: Wenxue guji kanxingshe, 1955), 1:110.

14. As with all Chinese names, we follow the original order of surname (Zhang) then personal name (Yingyu). Zhang Yingyu 張應俞 was also known by the style name (*zi* 字) Kuizhong 夔衷.

15. According to Wu Zhaoyang, sixty-five stories have identifiable locales, of which thirty-eight are places in Fujian. Three additional stories feature protagonists from Fujian. See Wu Zhaoyang 吳朝陽, "*Dupian xinshu* Fujian difang shuxing kaoshu" 《杜騙新書》福建地方屬性考述, *Ming-Qing xiaoshuo yanjiu* 明清小說研究 113, no. 3 (2014): 170–71.

16. On Fujian printing, see Lucille Chia, *Printing for Profit: The Commercial Publishers of Jianyang, Fujian (11th–17th Centuries)* (Cambridge, MA: Harvard University Asia Center, 2003). On the production and reception of popular works in the late Ming see He, *Home and the World*.

17. On commentary in Ming fiction, see David L. Rolston, *Traditional Chinese Fiction and Fiction Commentary: Reading and Writing Between the Lines* (Stanford: Stanford University Press, 1997). Of the two main forms of commentary, concluding commentary and interlinear/supralinear notes, Zhang uses the former almost exclusively; there are only a handful of brief interlinear notes that explain unfamiliar terms and concepts. His final comments are set off typographically by a line break and indentation; in most cases they open with the word *an* 按 ("I note").

18. "A Geomancer Uses His Wife to Steal a Good Seed" contains four more stories following the authorial commentary; one more story appears within the commentary on "Eating Human Fetuses to Fake Fasting." Only one story, not translated here, appearing in the "Marriage" section,

"Yin wa luchu mou qu qing" 因蛙露出謀娶情 ("A Marriage Scam of Passion Comes to Light Because of a Frog") lacks an author's comment.

19. For an overview of Ming history with a focus on these issues, see Timothy Brook, *The Confusions of Pleasure: Commerce and Culture in Ming China* (Berkeley: University of California Press, 1999).

20. See He, *Home and the World*, for examples of how late-Ming commercial publications mixed elements of classical and vernacular culture and of the extremely varied ways readers could engage with these books.

21. See Mark McNicholas, *Forgery and Impersonation in Imperial China: Popular Deceptions and the High Qing State* (Seattle: University of Washington Press, 2016), 98, 114.

22. This story is also unusual in containing internal explanatory notes defining rare words, a further hint of an origin elsewhere. Another story with both an internal moral and one in Zhang's comment is "Swindled on the Way Out of a Court Hearing."

23. A longer version of "A Marriage Scam of Passion Comes to Light Because of a Frog," involving a millionaire who drowns his neighbor in order to take the latter's wife as his concubine, only to have her abhor him when he confesses his crime years into their happy marriage, appears in chapter 7 of the story collection *Huanxi yuanjia* 歡喜冤家 (1630s), by Xihu yuyin zhuren 西湖漁隱主人.

24. Outside of *Kumo no taema amayo no tsuki* 雲妙間雨夜月, Bakin adapted at least five additional stories from the *Book of Swindles* into other works. See Itō Kanako 伊藤加奈子 et al., "Tohen shinsho" *yakuchū kō shohen* 「杜騙新書」訳注稿初編 (n.p., "Tohen Shinsho" no Kisoteki Kenkyū Purojekuto, 2015), 138 (and the extensive Japanese-language scholarship referenced there).

25. See Itō et al., "*Tohen shinsho*" *yakuchū kō shohen*, 138–41.

26. A facsimile reproduction of the Cunren tang edition (see below) appeared in Taiwan in a scholarly series with limited circulation, *Ming-Qing shanben xiaoshuo congkan chubian* 明清善本小說叢刊初編, which Tianyi chubanshe 天一出版社 began publishing in Taipei in 1985 (individual volumes are undated). For other facsimile reproductions, see the bibliography.

27. For a list of major modern editions of *Dupian xinshu*, see the bibliography.

28. Ding Xiaoshan 丁曉山, ed., *Fang pian jing* 防騙經 (Beijing: Zhongguo wenlian chubanshe, 1997). Some of the objectionable material that Ding excised was in the stories "A Geomancer Uses His Wife to Steal a Good Seed" and "A Eunuch Cooks Boys to Make a Tonic of Male Essence." In addition to translations into Modern Chinese, Ding's edition includes after some stories "contemporary explications" (*jinjie* 今解) featuring analogous swindles from contemporary China.

29. Youd, "Beyond *Bao*," and Roland Altenburger, "Täuschung und Prävention: Ambiguitäten einer Sammlung von Fallgeschichten aus der späten Ming-Zeit," in *Harmonie und Konflikt in China*, ed. Christian Soffel and Tilman Schalmey (Wiesbaden: Harrassowitz Verlag, 2014), 109–27.

30. These collections borrowed extensively from a wide variety of sources. A shorter, illustrated version of "Three Women Ride Off on Three Horses" appears, for example, as "A Donkey Owner Is Swindled" ("Lüfu shoupian" 驢夫受騙) in Lei Junyao 雷君曜, ed., *Huitu pianshu qitan* 繪圖騙術奇談 (Remarkable swindle tales, illustrated) (Shanghai: Saoye shanfang, 1909), vol. 1.

31. For details of these three copies, see the first section of the bibliography.

32. On Cunren tang, Juren tang, and the Yu family within the context of Jianyang publishing, see Chia, *Printing for Profit*, esp. 89, 377n140.

33. The close connection between the two editions is apparent from the relationship between the illustrations and the 1617 preface by Xiong Zhenji. The illustrations are keyed to allusions that appear in the preface but nowhere else in the book, making them thoroughly opaque without that context—yet no single early copy that we have seen contains both. The images appear on the first page of *juan* 1 to 4 in the two copies (Harvard and Tokyo) of the Cunreng tang edition that we have seen, which both lack the preface. The National Archives manuscript, by contrast, includes the preface but not the illustrations, which are likely to have been present in the imprint on which it is based but left out by the copyists.

34. For example, within the National Archives copy, the title of the collection appears in Xiong Zhenji's preface as *Jianghu qiwen dupian xinshu* 江湖奇聞杜騙新書 and in the table of contents as *Xinke Jianghu lilan dupian xinshu* 新刻江湖歷覽杜騙新書. The title at the head of each *juan* is slightly different, *Dingke Jianghu lilan dupian xinshu* 鼎刻江湖歷覽杜騙新書; the same discrepancy recurs in the Cunren tang edition. The first page of the main text also identifies a second publisher, (Zhang Huaigeng 張懷耿, *zi* Hanchong 漢冲); this is effaced in the Cunren tang edition. Another glaring inconsistency is the numbering of the twenty-four category headings: in the first two *juan* they are unnumbered, but numbering begins in the third *juan*—and is erroneous (Type 14 should be Type 15). The editors apparently realized their slipup when compiling the table of contents, whose count is accurate, but did not correct the misnumbering in the text proper.

   For a comparison of various editions, see Niu Jianqiang 牛建強, "Wan Ming duanpian shiqing xiaoshuoji *Dupian xinshu* banbenkao" 晚明短篇世情小說集《杜騙新書》版本考, *Wenxian jikan* 文獻季刊 3 (July 2000): 200–10.

The Book of Swindles

Type 1

Misdirection and Theft

Stealing Silk with a Decoy Horse

Chen Qing, a man from Jiangxi province, often traveled to Nanjing to sell horses on Three Mountains Street, in front of the Temple of Granted Wishes.[1]

Once, when he had in his possession a fine silver-colored horse worth some forty ounces of silver, he was approached by a man who walked with a graceful gait, carried an expensive-looking umbrella, and was dressed in resplendent attire.[2] This crook—for so he was—stopped in his tracks and stared at the horse as if he couldn't tear himself away from it.

"How much would you part with that horse for?" he asked.

"Forty ounces of silver," Chen replied.

"I'll buy it," the crook said, "but we'll have to go to my house to draw up a contract and weigh out the silver."

"Where do you live?"

"Hongwu Gate."

With that, the crook mounted the silver horse and set off, with Chen riding another horse behind him. Halfway through their journey, the crook spotted a silk shop. He dismounted, put his umbrella down outside a nearby tavern, and told Chen: "Watch my things while I purchase a few bolts of silk. I'll be back in a moment."

This guy must be rich, Chen thought. *He'll be able to close the deal on the horse for sure.*

The crook went into the shop and made a show of haggling. When the proprietor accused him of demanding an unreasonable price, the crook lied: "Allow me to show it to a colleague before I respond to your offer."

"You're welcome to show these fine goods to anyone you wish, just don't go far."

"My horse and man are right there. What are you worried about?"

Once he had the silk in hand, the crook slipped out the door and fled. Seeing that the horse and servant were still there, the proprietor was unconcerned. Chen waited until noon and, when the man still didn't return, concluded that he must be a crook. Picking up the umbrella, he mounted the silver horse and started leading the other horse back to the stables.

The silk vendor ran over and stopped him. "Your partner took my silk. Where are you going?"

"What partner?"

"The man who rode here with you just now. Don't play dumb. You'd better give me back my silk."

"I have no idea what rock that fellow crawled out from under. All I know is that he said he wanted to buy my horse and was taking me to his house to get the money. That's why we came here together. He told me he was going to buy some silk from your shop and we'd be on our way shortly. I've been waiting a long time and he hasn't shown up, so I'm heading back to the stables. Don't get me mixed up in this."

"If he's not your partner, then why were you watching his umbrella and his horse? I only let him take the silk because I saw you and the horses here. The two of you conspired to steal my silk!"

The two argued to an impasse and ended up bringing their dispute to the Prefect of Yingtian.[3] First, the silk vendor gave his version of events. Chen then testified as follows: "I, Chen Qing, am originally from Jiangxi province, and I make my living as a horse trader. I often come to Three Mountains Street to sell horses at Weng Chun's shop. I've never done anything crooked! I happened to meet a man who expressed interest in buying a horse, and I traveled with him because he had to go home to get money to complete the purchase. Along the way, he stopped and went into this man's shop and then, unbeknownst to me, ran off with some silk. How does this make me a crook's accomplice?"

"That will do," the prefect said. "Bring the proprietor in for questioning and we'll get to the bottom of this."

The proprietor, Weng Chun, testified: "Chen often comes here to sell horses and stays at my place. He's an honest, law-abiding man."

"If he's so honest," the silk vendor asked, "what was he doing guarding the umbrella and horse of a crook? I won't believe him until I hear him explain that one."

"I was just watching his umbrella because he was buying a horse from me. I wasn't his accomplice."

"Did the man take the umbrella when he left?" the prefect asked.

"No," the silk vendor replied.

"He's a crook all right," said the prefect. "In order to steal your silk he feigned the purchase of a horse and used Chen Qing as security. Using someone else's horse to acquire your silk is the ruse known as 'obtaining passage through the state of Yu to attack the state of Guo.'[4] You're the one who fell for this scheme, so don't blame Chen."

Both were released with no restitution required.

It seems to me that even being a crook requires a lot of technique. This crook's method for stealing the silk was to say that he was buying a horse while doing nothing of the sort, but instead using the horse as a decoy.

This is why he was decked out in such finery in the first place: he wanted people to believe that he was a real millionaire. He stopped in his tracks and admired the horse to come across as a genuine buyer and maintained this pretense all the way to the silk shop. There, he lied about having a horse and an associate in order to convince the proprietor to trust him. As for making off with the silk, leaving his umbrella with Chen Qing, and getting Chen embroiled in a court case with the shop owner—these were all clever techniques to hoodwink the simple-minded. If it hadn't been for the prefect's discernment that this was a confidence scam of "attacking Guo through Yu," it would have led to what the Book of Changes calls "the calamity of a townsman being punished when a passerby takes an ox."[5] Even so, Chen could not avoid getting caught up in a court case and the vendor was conned in broad daylight. These moral degenerates are extremely crafty, so the gentleman needs to make his defenses airtight.[6] That way, however many tricks the common crook may have up his sleeve, you'll never be played for a fool.

Notes

1. Three Mountains Street in Nanjing was also the location of many publishing houses.
2. An umbrella was part of the standard regalia of a traveling government official, though the story does not suggest that this crook was trying to impersonate one.
3. Yingtian prefecture housed the southern, secondary capital of Nanjing.
4. This idiom, which means to borrow an associate's resources to attack one's true target, derives from events that took place in 658 B.C.E.
5. *Book of Changes*, third line of hexagram #25 (Wuwang 無妄).
6. Zhang Yingyu politely implies here and in other comments that his readers belong to the class of *junzi* 君子, "gentlemen," or people of cultural accomplishment and superior moral character.

Handing Over Silver Before Running Off with It

A man from Tongzhou named Su Guang dealt in fabric from Songjiang.[1] He and his son were halfway home from a sales trip to Fujian province, earnings in hand, when they encountered a man named Ji Sheng who claimed to be from another county in their home prefecture. His dialect was identical to theirs, and he too was on his way back from selling cloth in Fujian. Ji Sheng was a greenhorn. Seeing that Su Guang was from a neighboring town and that his financial resources were greater, he entrusted Su with twenty-odd ounces of his silver to store in Su's trunk. Su carefully carried it the whole way, with Ji's silver alongside his own as if the two men were partners.

After several days of travel, Ji saw a chance for profit and hatched a treacherous scheme. One night at an inn he pretended to have diarrhea and got out of bed repeatedly, opening and closing the door as he went in and out of the room. Little did he know that Su was an old hand: seeing Ji going in and out again and again, he became suspicious that Ji had some scheme in the works. *Moreover*, thought Su, *I'm not sure of his origins. While he does have twenty-odd ounces of silver stored in my trunk, tonight he seems to be up to no good.* The next time Ji stepped out, Su secretly got up and hid both his money and Ji's in a bundle of clothes, which he kept beside him in bed. He wrapped some bricks and stones in old clothing and placed these in the trunk. Then he feigned deep slumber.

Ji Sheng, seeing that Su Guang and his son had both fallen asleep, took the trunk and stole off into the night. Su lay in bed listening to Ji's movements. When he heard him leave and not return he said to himself, *Just as I thought—he was a crook. If he'd pulled this on anyone but me he'd have gotten away with it too.*

The next day when Su got up he made a show of being shocked at the discovery that Ji had stolen his silver and began tussling with the innkeeper.

"Your accomplice stole my money!" he said accusingly.

Su's son, unaware of his father's scheme, began to beat the innkeeper furiously, stopping only when his father whispered, "Everything's under control."

After breakfast, Su told his son, "I'm going to the county office to report this. If they catch that crook I'll need you to come along to testify; otherwise, they're sure to suspect that you took it and start asking questions." Su, certain that Ji would come back, had a plan of his own. They hurried homeward along back roads.

Ji, delighted at having stolen Su's money, wandered until midday, traveling nearly a hundred *li*. When he opened the trunk and discovered the bricks, stones, and old clothes, he stamped his feet in disgust and traveled all the way back to the inn, where he was roundly beaten by the innkeeper.

"You thief! You stole someone's money and got me involved too. You'll be strangled for this!" the innkeeper cursed, as he prepared to turn Ji over to the authorities. All Ji could do was blurt out the truth and beg for mercy by knocking his head on the ground. By then Su was several days' journey away—well out of reach. Ji was left to nurse his resentment.

Ji Sheng was no greenhorn businessman, but he was a greenhorn crook. First he entrusted his money to Su Guang, to keep the latter from being suspicious. Then he faked diarrhea by repeatedly opening and closing the door to their room and waiting for the others to fall asleep before he stole off with the money. His scheme was ingenious, to be sure: "giving temporarily in order to steal in the end" is a beguiling scam from the crooks' playbook. Little did he expect that Su was an old hand who would see right through him. Observing Ji's actions, he could tell what was on his mind. This is how Su was able to match him maneuver for maneuver and scheme for scheme. Ji was already being manipulated, he just didn't know it. He tried to turn another's property to his profit but ended up losing his own. A bright green greenhorn crook is no match for the seasoned man of the world! Later, when he went back to the inn, he was beaten and had to beg pathetically for mercy. There he was just making trouble for himself—and who was to blame for that? Ample proof that the principles of Heaven are clear as day.

Note

1. Tongzhou and Songjiang were both part of South Zhili. Tongzhou was a subprefecture (an administrative unit that contained several counties) within Yangzhou prefecture, close to the junction of the Grand Canal and the Yangzi River; Songjiang lay a short distance to the south.

A Clever Trick on a Pig Seller

Deng Zhaobao, from Jianyang in Fujian province, made his living as a roving peddler. One day, he was on his way to Da'an in Chong'an county to sell four piglets. When he reached the top of Ma'an Hill, he encountered a crook who told him he was interested in buying pigs. Deng thought: *Here we are on a remote mountain path with little traffic, far from any town. What's this guy doing trying to buy pigs?*

Warily, he asked where the man lived.

"Just up ahead, in Ma'an," the crook replied.

"If you want to buy, let's go complete the transaction at your house."

"But I'm on my way to the county seat. How about this: take one pig out of its cage so that I can inspect it. If it looks good, we can settle on a price, and I'll go home and weigh out the silver. Otherwise I'd be going out of my way for no reason."

This seemed reasonable, so Deng agreed and took out a pig to show him. Holding the pig by its tail, the crook put it on the ground and examined it closely. Then he intentionally released his grasp and the pig bolted. Feigning alarm, he cried out, "Oh no! Oh no!" and hurried after the pig in an attempt to retrieve it—or so it seemed. In fact, he was driving the pig away. Seeing the pig getting farther and farther afield, Deng recklessly sprinted after it. Little did he know that he was playing right into the hands of the crook, who watched Deng give chase. Once Deng was some two or three hundred paces away, the crook reached inside a cage and drew out another pig, then kicked over the other two cages. As the last two pigs scurried off, he hollered:

"Thank you kindly! Happy hunting!"

Deng wanted to go after him, but with three pigs on the loose he worried that he couldn't catch both pigs and thief. As the crook got farther and farther out of reach, Deng could only rail and curse. Fortunately, he was able to herd all three pigs back together and into their cages. Bitterly, he continued on his way.

It appears to me that this pig theft resulted from a chance encounter. Once the crook got the notion to steal, he used wily words to dupe Deng into trusting him. It was a case of "taking advantage of a man's own skills to cheat him." First of all, he released a pig and pretended to chase it in order to trick Deng into running off in pursuit. Next, he snatched a pig and kicked over the other cages to keep Deng from coming after him. In both cases, the oblivious man fell for an obvious ruse. A trap sprung just like that—what unparalleled cunning! Merchants, take note! It goes without saying that one must diligently guard against covert schemes, but even obvious traps demand vigilance.

Pilfering Green Cloth by Pretending to Steal a Goose

Once there was a large shop that did a bustling business in all sorts of fabric but was staffed solely by its owner. In a pen across the street a neighbor was raising a goose whose constant honking annoyed the proprietor so much that he was heard to say, "How I wish someone would steal that miserable creature and give me some peace and quiet."

A crook happened to overhear him, and came into the store on a slow business day. He raised his hands to salute the proprietor and then let them rest on a bolt of green cloth on a shelf.

"I won't lie to you," he said in a low voice. "I'm a petty thief, and I'd like to make a meal of that goose across the street. It won't be easy to snatch it from such a busy street, but I've got a plan, and I just need your help to pull it off."

"How can I help?" the proprietor asked.

"I'll be out here and I'll ask, 'Can I take it?' You stay inside and shout, 'Okay!' I'll ask again, 'Really?' And you answer again, 'Yes.

I've made up my mind: you can take it.' Then I'll be able to grab it without raising suspicions from anyone on the street. Go along with this and you'll be safe from thieves forever—you'll never have to lock your door again. But you've got to hide in the back and not peek out—the trick won't work if you're watching. You'll know I'm done when the goose stops honking. That's when you can come out."

The proprietor agreed, so they began their dialogue.

"May I take it?" the thief called out.

"Yes, go ahead," came the shout from within.

Another hollered question: "Really—I can take it?"

"I've made up my mind: you can take it."

The shopkeepers on either side heard the entire exchange, so when the thief left with a bolt of green cloth, they thought he was just borrowing it. Meanwhile, the proprietor hiding in his shop, still hearing the goose honk from time to time, didn't dare come out. The thief had long since made himself scarce. The goose went on honking and the proprietor kept on waiting, worrying all the while that no one was minding the shop. Eventually he came out and discovered that the goose was still there but a bolt of green cloth had disappeared from the shelf.

He canvassed the neighboring shops: "Did someone come into my shop just now and take a bolt of cloth?"

The shopkeepers answered, "Yes, it was that fellow who was asking about buying something. You kept telling him he could take it. He's long gone."

The proprietor, chagrined and embarrassed, said, "It looks like I've been well and truly scammed. I'll never live this down."

When the neighbors learned the whole story, they laughed at his foolishness and hailed the crook's ingenuity.

The gentleman is benevolent to the people and caring toward other creatures. That benevolence should first of all be extended to those in one's vicinity, and even a goose is a creature deserving of care. Can this shopkeeper be called "caring toward creatures" when he was so annoyed by the honking of a neighbor's goose that he wanted to see it stolen and killed? Where was his benevolent mind when he tried to profit from the disappearance of the goose and helped the crook steal it? This behavior enabled the eavesdropping crook to carry out his theft. The shopkeeper even abetted the theft. What a rat! Wanting to do away with someone else's goose, he ended up losing his own cloth. He brought this calamity upon himself and had no one else to blame. If you treat neighbors with benevolence and treat other creatures with due consideration, such a thing will never happen to you.

Type 2

The Bag Drop

Dropping a Bag by the Roadside to Set Up a Switcheroo

Jiang Xian, from Linchuan county in Jiangxi province, was a man of modest means.[1] Every year in the seventh month, following the early harvest, he would go to the Chong'an area in Fujian province to work as a cobbler. With the arrival of winter, having earned ten or so ounces of silver, he would head home with his savings. Once during the return trip Jiang happened to find a bag in the road. He picked it up and was overjoyed to discover that it contained several pieces of silver weighing two or three ounces.

Just as he was about to continue on his way, a passerby approached him. "I saw that! I deserve a share of the silver too. How about this: you keep it in your trunk for the time being, and when we find a quiet place, you can take it out to divvy up. Two thirds will go to you, since you picked it up, and one third to me since I witnessed the find."

Jiang was amenable to this arrangement, and given that the silver was going into his own trunk he had no reason to be suspicious.

Barely had they walked ten paces when another man came running up, looking distraught.

"I lost a bag with three ounces of silver in it," he cried. "I was going to use that money to pay my taxes. If you happen to have picked it up and would be kind enough to return it to me, Heaven will eternally reward your good deed."

The passerby put on a pitying expression. "This cobbler is in charge; he picked it up and was going to split the contents with me. Seeing as how you're clearly in dire straits, I'm willing to give up my share. You should offer him a modest reward and ask him to return the bag."

Exposed by this testimony, Jiang felt compelled to open his chest and let the man who had lost the silver retrieve his bag. Still, since he was receiving a little silver as a reward, he considered himself fortunate. Unbeknownst to him, the swindler took Jiang's own bag of silver and swapped in a decoy bag.

That night Jiang arrived in the Wushi area and used the reward money to treat himself to a drink. When he opened his big bag to put away his change, he discovered that it was filled with bars of copper and iron—not a speck of silver to be seen. All he could do was bewail his misfortune.

Before they prepared the decoy bag trap, these crooks must have spotted the silver Jiang had saved up. Lying in wait in an out-of-the-way place, one dropped the bag on the ground where the mark was certain to find it. He then emerged from his hiding place, asked to split the windfall, and had Jiang store the bag in the trunk that contained his own silver. The first crook later feigned sympathy and compelled Jiang to open his trunk and return the bag. But why did Jiang allow the man to retrieve the bag from the trunk himself? This gave the other crook the opportunity to substitute a decoy bag for the one containing Jiang's silver—Jiang didn't guard against the switcheroo! When Jiang picked up the silver he ought to have split it with the first man on the spot instead of putting it in his trunk. That's the mistake that caused him to fall for this scam. Then again, the two crooks had him in a remote location and would have robbed him of his silver regardless. This is why a traveler on the road doesn't seek ill-gotten gains and keeps his own property safely hidden. It's the only way to prevent loss.

Note

1. Linchuan was just south of the seat of Fuzhou prefecture.

Type 3

Money Changing

A Daoist in a Boat Exchanges Some Gold

Fei was a student at the National University in Nanjing. He was about to return home, as his term was ending, and he wanted to buy a few dozen ounces of high-grade gold as a present for his wife and concubines. Deng, a fellow National University student from the same county, urged him not to. "People who buy gold in the capital are often taken in by crooks who give them a piece of copper instead. If you don't need the gold in a hurry, why not buy it back home?"

"You can only get good gold in the capital," Fei replied. "If any crook could pull one over on me, I'd bow down to his skill."

Within a few days he had purchased more than ten ounces of gold, all at the going rate for purity and all of high quality. Later, he was approached by a young fellow who wanted to sell him a twelve-ounce ingot. Fei examined it, and it seemed to be pure, so he asked the price. "Since it's you asking, your honor," the fellow said, "I'd take a rate of five gold to one silver."

Fei handed the gold ingot to Deng to examine, thinking: *This gold could go for six, so five to one is more than fair.*

Deng looked it over and said, "It's good, all right. Close the deal now, and don't let him touch it again."

Fei paid with sixty ounces of silver and, as Deng had suggested, held onto the gold as he handed over the silver. The seller had no chance to pull a switcheroo—all he could do was take the money and go home.

The young seller went to see his father and explained how the two students had been so cautious that he'd had no chance to get the gold back. His father was distraught. "That was our family's entire livelihood! What're we supposed to live on now that you've given away our capital? Go find out quick when those students are leaving."

The son made inquiries and reported back that they had booked passage on a boat departing at such and such a day and time. At the scheduled time, the students boarded the boat and took their seats. They were shortly followed by the elder crook, disguised as a Daoist priest in an immaculate robe and hat. The captain welcomed this new passenger on board and struck up a conversation with him. The Daoist turned out to be an eloquent raconteur with an intimate knowledge of goings-on in the capital, both within officialdom and among the common people. The two students and the other passengers were happily drawn into the conversation.

Two days later, as dusk approached, the Daoist steered the conversation toward the appraisal of gems, jade, and jewels, and everyone chatted about that for a while. He then brought up the authentication of gold, remarking that he was an expert at distinguishing the counterfeit from the genuine. Fei bragged that he had paid a very favorable price for an ingot of pure gold in the capital. Several passengers asked him to show it to them so they could judge its purity. Smugly, Fei took it out and handed it around; everyone remarked enviously that the gold was fine indeed. By the time they had each taken a turn to examine it, the sky was getting dark. When they had given it back to Fei and he was about to return it to his trunk, the Daoist spoke up: "Might I take a look?"

Fei handed it over, and after examining it the Daoist handed the ingot back, saying, "It's pure gold, all right." As Fei put the gold away, the Daoist moved the conversation to a new topic. Soon, dinner was ready and everyone dispersed to eat. The next day, the Daoist paid his fare to the captain, bade farewell to the other passengers, and disembarked.

When Fei got home, he divided the gold among his wife and concubines. A few days later he called in a craftsman to make bracelets. Fei had him start with the small ingots, which the craftsman confirmed were all quality gold. Fei then boasted, "I also bought a twelve-ounce ingot that's even better."

The craftsman said, "The thing with the big ingots you get in the capital is that crooks tend to swap them out for copper ones."

"Look, I'll show you," said Fei. "No crook could pull one over on me."

The craftsman had no sooner picked it up than he laughed. "Yup, it's copper!"

Astounded, Fei snatched it back and examined it. "So it is. When Master Deng and I looked at it, it was definitely gold, and all the other passengers said so too. How could all of us have been fooled?"

Then the truth hit him. "Ah! Of course. The Daoist was the last one to look at it, and when he gave it back it was nearly dark and I didn't have a chance to examine it again before returning it to my trunk. That's when he switched it. But how could that Daoist have had a piece of copper that looked exactly like my ingot, to pull off such a seamless swap? I'd bet that young fellow in the capital who sold me the gold was the old crook's son. Since I didn't give him a chance to make the swap when he sold it, his dad must have followed me onto the boat to retrieve it."

People say that the old crook must have been a real pro to get Fei's gold. I disagree. Had Fei only kept it hidden away, even if the crook had possessed the clever stratagems of Zhuge Liang and the genius of Zhuang Zhou, he would have had no chance to handle that gold—and then how could he have stolen it? So the blame falls on Student Fei.[1] What a pity that he should bring this loss upon himself with his boasting!

Note

1. Zhuge Liang (181–234) served as prime minister of the state of Han during the Three Kingdoms period, and is known historically—and even more so in folklore—as a master strategist. Zhuang Zhou or Zhuangzi (369?–286? B.C.E.) was a thinker and writer. Both are associated with Daoism, Zhuang as a founder of Daoist philosophy and Zhuge as the student of a Daoist priest; popular portrayals show him in the robe of a Daoist priest and holding a fan made from the feathers of a heavenly crane.

Type 4

Misrepresentation

Forged Letters from the Education
Intendant Report Auspicious Dreams

Most of the top successful candidates in the 1600 provincial civil service examinations in Fujian were students of Master Shen.[1] Master Shen was, as a result, widely revered among the populace.

By the beginning of the twelfth month, all the holders of the provincial *juren* degree had gone to sit for the metropolitan examinations in Beijing. Meanwhile, back in the capital of Fujian, a crook hatched a scheme for which he recruited a local-level degree holder, a *xiucai*, who was from the same prefecture and had a good hand for calligraphy. The scheme involved composing fraudulent letters in Master Shen's name, sealing them up with a stamp, and having the swindler deliver one to the family of each new *juren*.

When the swindler arrived at each house, he would tell the family, "Master Shen has written a letter and dispatched your servant to deliver it posthaste. He also entrusted me with the message that the young master of your noble house is certain to triumph in the coming year's examinations. The master foresaw this in a remarkable dream and ordered me here to share the good tidings beforehand—with the caution that this news must be kept in the strictest confidence. Young Master So-and-So lives near your honorable residence, and Master Shen fears that if he were to learn that you received a special messenger he'd accuse the master of playing favorites. Master Shen is sending a letter of greeting to that house as well, but it's just for appearances' sake—nothing special."

Arriving at the next house, the swindler would say the same thing: he'd come on express purpose and the other visits he was making were just for show. When the recipient opened and read the letter, he saw characters written in exquisite calligraphy and lines of marvelous literary subtlety. Each letter related an auspicious dream containing an omen indicating that the candidate would rank first in the national examinations. Some omens derived from the candidate's name, others from the name of his place of origin. Each prediction was supposedly based on words that had appeared in a dream of Master Shen.

I once saw the letter for provincial-level degree holder Xiong Shaozu, which read:

Fujian is home to more talented men than any other province in the realm, the number of graduates often surpassing even Zhejiang and the capital itself. Yet none of these talented men approaches the depth and erudition of your master's command of the *Spring and Autumn Annals*, nor the vigor and breathtaking acuity of his prose. Next spring will bring triumph in the examinations at the Ministry of Rites—this is a certainty I arrived at without recourse to divination. On the twenty-second day of the eleventh lunar month, around midnight, I dreamed of a flying bear [*xiong*] holding in its paw a red spring blossom, which it lifted high above its head. As it passed in front of a red sun, I saw two gilded characters: First Place. So clearly did they appear to me that I remembered them after I awoke. The sun represents the district of Jianyang, the literal meaning of which is "sun maker." Bear, Xiong, is your master's surname. The spring blossoms signify your master's comprehensive and dazzling command of the *Spring and Autumn Annals*. The gilded characters First Place are a distinct and auspicious omen. Your master's talent and my dream together provide clear evidence that he will be the top examination candidate in the realm. The possibility that one of my disciples should be the First Place winner delighted me so much that I was unable to sleep and dispatched a special messenger to share the news—please keep it in confidence.

Xiong's family members were overjoyed to read this and tipped the messenger three ounces of silver. When he asked for more, they tipped him another two ounces, saying: "Upon next year's triumph, we'll tip you another ten."

Virtually every letter reported an auspicious dream of this type and earned its bearer a tip of several ounces of silver. The next year, the exam candidates who'd had their wings clipped in the capital flew south. When they would meet up, each would tell the story of the letter containing Master Shen's dream. The listener would invariably clap his hands and laugh uproariously. "Quite the spring dream! That crook is a genius if ever there was one. Who wouldn't have been gulled into happily paying him?"

All told, the crook's takings totaled over a hundred ounces of silver. I've related this story for a laugh.

This crook managed to pull off a remarkable swindle with these new provincial-exam graduates: the painless scam. Although the graduate's family members paid out a tip of a few ounces of silver, the scam made his entire household happy for four months. It's a pity that the swindler hasn't returned to scam again; if he did, people would still be happy to tip him. It's the most ingenious swindle of all.

Note

1. The text refers to the *gengzi* year in the sixty-year Chinese calendrical cycle, which during the reign of the Wanli emperor would be 1600 C.E. This story mentions two historical personages by name. Master Shen is likely Shen

Jingkai 沈儆炌 (*jinshi* 1589), who served as a vice commissioner of education (*duxue fushi* 督學副使) in Fujian during the Wanli period. Xiong Shaozu, a letter to whom Zhang Yingyu quotes in the story, is one of four men from Jianning prefecture in Fujian (which includes Jianyang) whose names appear on the list of successful *juren* for the year 1600; all four failed to pass the metropolitan examination in 1601. Wu Zhaoyang speculates that Xiong Shaozu may have been related to Xiong Zhenji, who wrote the 1617 preface to the first edition of the *Book of Swindles*. See Wu Zhaoyang, "*Dupian xinshu* Fujian difang shuxing kaoshu," 168–70.

Using Broom Handles to Play a Joke on Sedan Bearers

The overland post route from the capital of Fujian province to Jian Brook stretches a distance of one hundred and twenty *li*. The usual fare for the trip by sedan chair is only sixteen hundredths of an ounce of silver. When travelers are sparse the price drops to fourteen, and sometimes sedan bearers will even carry for a mere twelve. But once the fare is in their hands, the sedan bearers will take passengers just five *li* or so before setting them down. Or, upon reaching the slightest incline, they'll set the chair down and refuse to go any farther. Most people end up riding the first two thirds of the way and walking the final third—virtually every traveler has been ensnared by them.

During examination season and when candidates are on their way home, the price can go as high as twenty-four, but no less than twenty. The bearers always insist that the silver for their fare be weighed out and paid in advance. Having pocketed the money, they'll carry for no more than twenty *li* before subcontracting to another porter, slashing down what was a reasonable fare so that they themselves retain half the money. These subcontracted sedan bearers in turn only go five *li* before plunking the chair down and complaining that they weren't paid the going rate. With no alternative, the scholar will cough up again. But scholars pass through relatively infrequently and they never haggle.

A certain government clerk often traveled along this road and had been repeatedly fleeced by these sedan bearers. One day, while preparing to set out yet again for the county seat, he composed a satirical quatrain on two strips of paper and wrapped a large square of paper around them. Then he took two old broom handles, sawed them to the same length, and wrapped them in rolls of tissue paper so that they resembled two bolts of silk. The next day, the sedan bearers saw him setting off on his own and vied for his business.

The clerk told them, "I've been called home on an urgent matter and don't have any cash on me. I'm prepared to pay twenty and foot the bill for food and wine tonight and tomorrow morning. But paying ready cash now or subcontracting to other porters is out of the question."

Two porters were willing to take the job and began trussing the two packages onto the sedan chair.

"Secure them safely and don't let them get damaged!" the clerk warned them. Climbing into the sedan chair, he added, "When we get to Muslim Kiln Street I'll need to mail an important letter. Don't forget when we get there."

They arrived at Muslim Kiln Street in the early afternoon.

"Wait here for a moment while I go mail the letter. I'll be right back."

In fact, the clerk fled back home via a secondary road.

After they'd waited longer than it takes to eat a meal and he still wasn't back, the two porters conferred.

"While we were carrying him he said he wouldn't be gone long. We've got two bolts of silk here. Why keep waiting? Let's skedaddle!"

With that they raced off, arriving home around dusk. One suggested that they take a bolt of silk apiece. The other insisted that they settle up later in case one was worth more. Back home, they unwrapped the tissue paper to discover that each bolt contained only a sawed-off old broom handle. They were accompanied by a square package, which they supposed contained letters. Opening it, the porters saw a piece of paper with the following words written in a large hand:

> You porters are a tricky lot,
> but now you've fallen for my plot;
> unless I'd handled both you dolts
> I would have lost my silk—two bolts!

"Bloody crook! Bloody, brilliant crook!" The house rang with their curses.

Overhearing the noise, other sedan bearers from the neighborhood came in and asked who this crook was they were cursing. When they told the story of what had happened, their neighbors roared with laughter. Going back outside, they attached the broom handles to a fence so that they stuck out halfway and pasted the poem between them. Every passerby who read the poem and saw the broom handles burst out laughing. "That clerk had you good and proper. You two porters shouldn't have conspired to cheat him. It's your own fault, and you deserve to be publicly mocked for being handled like the dumb old brooms you are. If it really were silk that you'd stolen, you wouldn't want word getting out and that officer coming after you, would you? You have only yourselves to blame, so don't go cursing him!"

Three days later, the clerk returned. Seeing the poems still pasted on the fence, he asked a local, "A few days ago two sedan bearers stole a couple of bolts of silk that I was carrying for someone. Do you happen to have heard anything about that?"

Realizing that this was the clerk who had played the joke on the sedan bearers, the person responded, "If you don't go looking for your silk, they won't dare come looking for their fare!"

The clerk burst out laughing and went on his way.

This clerk who hitched a free ride wasn't the crook; the two sedan bearers were the crooks. If the clerk were a crook, would he have come back making inquiries? And when he did, why did the sedan bearers not dare show their faces? This is called using the crook's tricks against him—ingenious! Be that as it may, if you ever have to hire sedan bearers or porters when traveling, hire them through your innkeeper. He can track them down if necessary, so there's no risk of their absconding with your property.

Type 5

False Relations

Inciting a Friend to Commit Adultery and Swindling Away His Land

Bi Ho,[1] from Shanxi province, was a treacherous schemer, a man full of secret vendettas and malicious intrigues. Everyone in town had been harmed by him. His younger cousin Bi Song owned a plot of land worth over fifty ounces of silver that bordered on Ho's fields. Ho had schemed several times to acquire the plot without success, so he forged a false friendship with Song, frequently treating him to meals and entertainments. Amusing themselves together at all hours, the two became as inseparable as brothers.

In the same town lived a stubborn man with a violent temper named Lin Yuan. His wife, née Luo, was a beautiful and licentious woman who had come to despise her husband. Ho took advantage of the couple's falling out to seduce Ms. Luo and begin an affair. Ostensibly the affair was to be clandestine, but actually Ho wanted Song to know about it, so he intentionally left clues that led Song to figure out what was going on.

Song admonished Ho: "Some friend you are! Such a beautiful woman—let me sleep with her once, why don't you? Has the gal ensnared your heart?"

"You couldn't handle a woman this passionate," Ho demurred. "If I brought you along, you'd become infatuated for sure. I'm worried that you'd start coming and going at all hours and end up getting discovered. If her husband found out, your life would be over."

Song, however, suspected that Ho simply wanted to monopolize Ms. Luo's favors, so he secretly seduced Ms. Luo, who quickly acquiesced. Passion bound them tighter and tighter. As soon as her husband left on a trip, she would invite either Ho or Song—sometimes all three would share a bed, their passion uniting them as one.

After about a month, Ho secretly informed on the other two to Luo's husband.

"I recently learned that Brother Song has become romantically involved with your wife. I know him well and have told him to stop several times, but he ignores me. I'm sure you'll want to catch him in the act. But if you succeed, don't beat him too hard. He'll definitely ask me to intercede on his behalf, and to make sure he stops this foolishness I'll insist that he give you some extra silver. Just be careful not to kill him."

He left Lin Yuan bursting with rage.

The next day, Lin told his wife that he had to go on a trip that would last at least three days. Song watched as Lin departed. Having asked around and learned that Lin had gone off on a trip, he threw himself into Luo's arms and took her into the bedroom for a romp. Lin sprang from his hiding place and into the bedroom, where he found the two lovers naked on the bed. Lin hauled Song to the floor and began pummeling him. Luo, however, restrained her husband with all her might, so Lin wasn't able to beat him too badly.

Song begged Lin to release him. "I'll pay you!" he promised.

"Who'll be your guarantor?" Lin asked.

"Call my cousin, Ho."

Lin agreed and sent someone to fetch Ho. When Ho arrived, he admonished Song: "See where your wayward behavior has led you? You should be calling your brother to bail you out, not me!"

Song replied, "Don't get my brother involved. Just front me the ransom money and I'll pay you back the day after tomorrow."

Ho answered, "I can negotiate on your behalf, but you put me in an awkward spot about paying. I do see that this is an emergency, and if I don't front the money I won't be able to talk you out of this predicament. But in that case you'll need to put up something tangible as a guarantee."

Song duly offered to sell him the deed to the adjoining plot of land.

"Sell at a low price." Ho advised him. "If it's too high, the money will go to Lin Yuan anyway."

They settled on a price of forty ounces of silver. Ho returned home and retrieved thirty ounces, which he handed to Lin.

"I demand sixty," Lin declared.

Ho replied, "The redemption price applies to both adulterers, meaning that half the price is for the woman. Your wife, moreover, is such a beauty that she'd be worth sixty ounces on her own. You're already getting half price."

Despite further appeals, however, Lin refused to budge on his demand.

Ho told him: "Song's fields are worth forty ounces of silver, and I don't have ready cash. How about if you wait a month and then I'll give you another ten ounces."

When Lin demanded a promissory note, Ho told him: "If anyone else had handled this negotiation they'd have received a twenty-percent commission. I deserve eight ounces of silver for putting this matter to rest for you as it is, and here you are pressing me for an I.O.U.!"

In the end, Lin released Song without a promissory note.

Several days later, Song brought forty-four ounces of silver, which included the interest on the original value of his land, to redeem the title deed to his fields, but Ho refused to sell it back to him. A month later, Lin came to Ho asking for the promised money, and Ho told him: "I showed you how to make thirty ounces of silver—are these few ounces more than my services deserve?"

Later, Lin told other people the story of how Ho had taught him to catch the adulterers. Only then did Song realize that Ho had sold him out. By then, however, he had already fallen into Ho's trap, and it was too late for regrets.

Ho's scheme was to acquire Song's field by luring him into adultery, and it was to incite this adultery that Ho befriended him in the first place. He also made sure that the incitement wasn't obvious, so that Song appeared to fall into fornication of his own accord. As for the plot of land he coveted, he bided his time until Song was in distress and then obtained it in a leisurely fashion by intervening to resolve his dilemma. Truly a brilliant scheme! So long as he was expecting a future payoff, Lin Yuan was sure not to reveal its origins. The treachery of a false friend like Ho is too deep to fathom. That's why, in dealing with people of habitually immoral conduct, one must keep them from getting too close.

Note

1. This name would normally be written "He" in pinyin romanization; it is given here as "Ho" to avoid confusion with the English pronoun.

Type 6
Brokers

A Conniving Broker Takes Paper and
Ends Up Paying with His Daughter

Shi Shouxun, a native of Da'an in Fujian province, was from a wealthy family that manufactured and distributed paper. One day he packed over a thousand bales of paper, worth more than eight hundred ounces of silver, and headed to Suzhou to sell it.

He went through the shop of Weng Bin'er, a resident broker. Weng had amassed sizable debts to previous clients, so when this apparent greenhorn, Shi, came along Weng decided to use Shi's paper to repay them. He then bluffed Shi, keeping him cooling his heels for half a year.

Shi's family sent to Suzhou another five hundred-plus bales of paper, which Weng sold for cash on Shi's behalf. But even after receiving these proceeds he continued to string Shi along with excuses that his funds had all gone to pay off old accounts. After waiting another half a year, Shi finally realized that he'd been taken in and angrily lambasted Weng. Weng, having nothing to say in response, turned for help to his relative Liu Guangqian. Liu advised

Weng to write Shi a promissory note for eight hundred ounces of silver and then urge him to return home for the time being.

The following year Shi brought more paper to Suzhou; Weng sold it for him but was still unable to repay the earlier debt. Shi was again kept waiting for half a year. During that time Shi noticed that Weng's daughter, Yunying, was both attractive and unattached. Figuring that he was unlikely to get his money, he engaged Liu Guangqian to act as matchmaker and inquire about making Yunying his concubine in return for the cancellation of Weng's debt. Weng happily agreed, but Yunying, who was just fifteen years old, refused. Weng and his wife went to her room to cajole her: "In ancient times Tiying volunteered to become a government slave to save her father from punishment.[1] Now, your father owes this client eight hundred ounces of silver, and you'd be clearing that obligation. Besides, these Fujian merchants are flush. Should you bear him a son, you'll get a share of his fortune and live in the lap of luxury." Yunying finally consented.

At the time of their marriage, Shi was over sixty years old, and before four years had gone by he returned to Fujian and passed away. Even before Yunying's period of customary mourning for her husband was over, Weng had married his daughter to another man. She became a concubine to one Liang Enci of Lishui county in Nanjing, following an engagement gift of a hundred ounces of silver to Weng.

Shi Shouxun's son, Qin, got wind of this, and when he traveled to Suzhou that year with a load of paper he went to pay his respects to the Wengs, addressing Weng Bin'er as "maternal grandfather," but Weng snubbed him. Qin then asked to meet his father's concubine, but she refused to receive him. His fellow merchants were incensed and cried out, "Your father gave an engagement gift of eight hundred ounces, and yet, before they would even have been married for four years, she was remarried to someone else. What would be the harm in letting you see her this one time? Their behavior is unconscionable! You should sue."

So Qin lodged a complaint with Metropolitan Inspector Cai. Weng Bin'er, however, was not in the least intimidated. With the

Shis as in-laws he could ride high on his family's restored prestige; moreover, he was sitting on over a thousand ounces of silver. Arguments dragged on for nearly two years in various administrative offices and circuit courts, whose officers all took bribes from both parties and made a series of ill-founded judgments. Ultimately, Shi Qin had to petition the Ministry of Justice to obtain the following decision:

> Weng Bin'er used his daughter to pay back eight hundred ounces of silver—nearly the price of the famous beauty Lüzhu.[2] But whereas Shi Shouxun agreed to this engagement gift, we pass no judgment on it. Subsequently, before her mourning was completed, Weng remarried her to Merchant Liang and pocketed a substantial sum; in doing so he treated his daughter as a commodity, in contravention of the law. He shall receive a total of thirty blows of the rod, and is hereby ordered to transfer to Shi Qin the one hundred ounces of silver he received from Liang, along with the fifty ounces worth of clothing and jewelry that Shi Shouxun provided to Yunying.

As a result of these protracted proceedings, Weng Bin'er's family nearly went bankrupt and fell into poverty.

Conniving intermediaries are second only to itinerant crooks in the harm they cause with their thieving swindles. When itinerant crooks plot to take things covertly, that's burglary; when conniving intermediaries swindle away goods to sell openly, that's robbery. Both constitute a type of theft. The perils of dealing with brokers are legion. They go behind their clients' backs to use the goods they bring in for all sorts of underhanded deals. They often steal from their suppliers, and they invariably use the stock of one client to pay off debts to another. Such behavior is the impoverished broker's stock in trade. Shi Shouxun tumbled into this pitfall because he failed to perform due diligence in selecting a broker. One must be picky. Likewise, someone should have stopped him from setting his sights on the daughter. How many years does a man over sixty have left, and what good could come of taking a concubine so far from home? This left it to his son to sort things out, at not inconsiderable expense, and even though he ended up winning in court, it was far from complete restitution. How deplorable that the wicked blackguard Weng Bin'er would trade his daughter for eight hundred silver—that in itself was beyond the pale. But then he went on to bring another son-in-law into his family. If he did want to marry his daughter off a second time, he should at least have returned the personal gifts to Shi's son so as to avoid further trouble. But no, his avarice was insatiable, and it bankrupted his family. This is truly a parable of the consequences of duplicity and immorality.

Notes

1. Tiying (fl. 167 B.C.E.) was famous as a dutiful daughter who saved her father from execution by offering herself as a palace slave.
2. Lüzhu (d. 300) was a famously talented and beautiful woman whom the official Shi Chong (249–300) purchased as a concubine for three bushels of pearls.

A Destitute Broker Takes Some Wax to
Pay Off Old Debts

Zhang Ba was from Sichuan province. A quick-witted and conscientious fellow, he was tall and gutsy to boot. One day he bought
over a hundred crateloads of wax and headed to Jianning prefecture in Fujian province to sell them at Broker Qiu's shop. Qiu had
fallen on hard times, and although he managed to maintain the
appearance of wealth he was in fact deeply in debt, having failed
to repay several dealers for their goods. When Zhang Ba showed
up with his wax, Qiu behaved like the crook he was and entered it
into his ledger under fictitious names instead of under Zhang's. He
promised to pay Zhang soon, but a few days later Zhang was stroll-
ing down the street when what did he see but his own wax for sale
in one store after another! He asked who the supplier was, and the
consignment records all bore different names.

Suspecting some duplicity afoot, Zhang Ba went back to Qiu's
store and confronted the broker. "You took my wax and used it to

repay other accounts. I want the details on each and every one. Tell me the truth or you'll find yourself talking to my fists."

Broker Qiu went mute and couldn't answer. Zhang flew at him with his fists and collared him like a hawk seizing a sparrow. Then he kicked Qiu around like a football.

Qiu cried for mercy: "You're too clever for me, my lord! I admit that I gave your wax to other merchants to settle old accounts and sold some for living expenses. But at this point I can't ask all those vendors to give it back."

Zhang said, "Make an account entry for every bit of wax you used to pay others back and for every crate the stores are selling. Indicate that it's all on consignment and you haven't been paid for any of it. I'll take your ledger in to lodge a complaint, and, with you giving staunch testimony on my behalf, we'll just see if those stores don't return my product."

Broker Qiu did as he was told and wrote accounts receivable entries for everything. Zhang took the ledger straight to the county office to open a case with Venerable Mei, the acting magistrate. After reading the complaint, Mei tossed it to the ground and denied it. Zhang was devastated at the prospect of losing his capital and broke down in tears. He desperately pleaded his case until Venerable Mei finally allowed it to proceed and sent runners to check the wax in the stores.

Zhang bribed these clerks with silver and they reported back, "All the stores have wax with Zhang Ba's seal mark."

"How could they take the wax on consignment and not pay him?" Venerable Mei responded. He thereupon issued a summons.

The shop owners conferred amongst themselves outside the office: "We all bought some of Zhang's wax and paid Qiu in full, and now that broker is trying to collect for it *again*. Besides, Qiu was using some of that wax to pay off his debts to us; where does he get off demanding that we compensate him for escrow payments that *he* owed? The lot of us ought to pool our money to cover the cost of an inducement, and then go explain our situation and have our day in court."

They collected a hundred ounces of silver, which they offered to a relative of Venerable Mei who lived nearby. Now Venerable Mei was an upstanding official, and he couldn't be swayed. Instead he had the merchants brought in for trial. One of them, from the Jiang family store, had experience with lawsuits. He opened his case by saying, "Broker Qiu sold us the wax in a fair and equitable exchange. How could Zhang Ba again demand payment from us if the broker failed to compensate him fully? So the broker's fallen on hard times—that's got nothing to do with us."

"I didn't sell them the wax," Qiu testified. "Rather, I had some accounts due to these stores, and when Zhang Ba's wax came in they falsely offered to take it on consignment and pay me within a few days. But once the wax was in their hands they just counted it against what I owed them. I certainly had no intention of tricking my client out of his money."

Venerable Mei addressed the shopkeepers: "If Qiu owed you money, you should have sought restitution from him. How could you have appropriated his client's goods to cover his personal obligations to you? The rest of you will have to compensate Zhang if you want to avoid criminal charges."

Merchant Jiang, who had bribed Venerable Mei's relative, pressed their case that it was a fair and equitable exchange and unrelated to any outstanding debt. Venerable Mei grew angry and punished Jiang with ten strokes of the rod. Jiang insisted and was rewarded with another twenty strokes. This terrified the others, who said they were willing to pay restitution and make peace. Jiang was imprisoned as surety, and the wax had to be paid for within three days or else he would be punished further. By the third day they had come up with the money and paid Zhang in full. Zhang was so grateful for Mei's grace that before leaving he burned incense to show his respect and prostrated himself before the magistrate's office.

Life is precarious when one is abroad on business. Far from familiar ties, one becomes dependent on intermediaries to serve as one's eyes and ears. If you happen to find a fair and honest broker, your goods will be taken care of. But should he be wily and corrupt, your goods and compensation alike will be imperiled. So picking a good intermediary is a vital business decision—one not to be taken lightly! If he's plainspoken and forthright, that means he's fair and honest. But if, when you first meet, he visibly sizes you up before taking you into his confidence, that's a sign of a wily, conniving mind. If you're getting close to negotiating a price but the counteroffers are a long time in coming, he surely has some kind of scam in mind. If his rooms are not just neat and tidy but excessively showy, he's likely to be an ostentatious and inattentive person who is unable to get things done. If his clothes are patched and dirty, or if he looks lowly and devious, with a stooped posture and hungry eyes, or if his headgear is ill suited to the season, he's surely an impoverished sort. If he favors natty attire or his dress and appearance are otherwise unusual, chances are he's not well established but in fact from a penniless household. If, on the other hand, his clothes are not showy and he wears only plain cloth, don't assume that he's poor—this is a man of reliable character. A merchant who understands these principles could never be taken in by a broker the way Zhang Ba was. Save for upright Venerable Mei choosing to listen to his plea, Zhang would have returned home empty-handed. Hence I record this to show merchants the only way to remain safe from worries: be scrupulous from the outset about the intermediaries you employ to distribute your goods.

Type 7

Enticement to Gambling

A Stern Warning to a Gambler Provokes
Others to Entice Him to Relapse

Zhang Shisheng, from Juxi in Fujian province, was the spoiled son of a rich family. His father divided his fortune evenly among him and his brothers. The family's land was fertile and productive, and they had only to sit back and reap its rewards. When Zhang's father died, around the time when Wanli coins had just entered circulation,[1] Zhang was lured into gambling by a group of hoodlums. As the immature scion of a millionaire he was enthralled by the hedonistic pleasures of drinking and revelry in the gambling hall. Being a careful steward of his wealth was the furthest thing from his mind! Within a few months he had lost several hundred ounces of silver, yet he carried on blithely gambling away with no intention of stopping.

In the same town lived a certain Chen Rongyi, whom Zhang's father had employed as a foreman overseeing servants. Though a rather coarse fellow, he was loyal and couldn't stand to see Zhang being corrupted by crooks. So he prepared a lavish banquet at which

Zhang was the sole guest. As they ate and drank, he gradually brought the conversation around to the topic of what things had been like when Zhang's father was alive. He explained to Zhang how his father had worked all his life for his money, where his wealth had come from, and how scrupulous his father had been about saving and spending. He praised Zhang for being a capable man and expressed sympathy at how hard things must be for him. He also talked about trends in contemporary society, including the difficulties of making a living nowadays and how hard life is for the poor.

He then gave Zhang a piece of advice: "It wasn't easy for your honorable father to earn his fortune. Keep in mind how diligently he worked and be a good custodian of the family legacy. You need to stop gambling. You've already gambled away a few hundred ounces of silver, but never mind that—what's gone is gone. If you turn over a new leaf now, you'll live just as comfortably as before."

Chen spoke so earnestly that Zhang's conscience was momentarily stirred, and he promised: "I'll do just as you say. I vow never to gamble again."

Sure enough, the next day when the hoodlums invited him out gambling, he turned them down. At first they were all surprised; later they figured out that it was because of Chen's advice. At a loss for what to do, they talked it over and came to an agreement: "Whoever can entice him back to gambling gets ten ounces of silver."

"I can do it," volunteered a certain Chai Kun, so the other gamblers chipped in to make a sealed packet with ten ounces of silver.

Chai saw Zhang sitting idly in a roadside pavilion and sidled up to him. He chatted about this and that for a while before asking, "I heard that you've given up gambling. Is it true?"

"Yes."

"Gambling's bad. You're a brave man to be able to stop on your own like that. I'm really impressed that the scion of such a rich and illustrious family could be so wise. There's just one thing: the word on the street is that you only quit after Old Chen urged you to. Is that so?"

"That's right, he did give me some advice."

Chai Kun gave a disappointed sigh. "Chen used to be a young lout who ran around with a bad crowd. If it hadn't been for your father and your uncles, there would've been nothing to check his degenerate ways. Now, you're the scion of a prominent family and a smart man besides. Are you going to listen to the chidings of such a base character and let word get out that you're taking your cues from him? Every man on the street will be laughing at you behind your back— they'll say you're not the master of your own affairs. The way I see it, you'd be better off doing a little gambling for another fortnight or two, then quitting of your own accord. That way people would say that you'd lost your taste for gambling, not that you're taking orders from a disreputable character. That's what a real man would do, and you'd be protecting the reputation of your late father's house."

Zhang was a gullible greenhorn; hearing this glib speech, he reckoned, *He's right. If I stop now, everyone will say it's at Chen's behest. I should gamble for another month and then quit on my own. That'll show 'em I'm a real man!* Before long, he was back at it in the gambling hall. Chai Kun, meanwhile, left with his payoff from the gamblers. After another month of gambling, Zhang's appetite for the game was as strong as ever. Chen spoke with him again, but this time his words fell on deaf ears. In the end, Zhang bankrupted his family, all due to Chai's disastrous provocation.

The only reason Zhang Shisheng would be gulled by Chai Kun's absurd propositions and reject Chen Rongyi's loyal advice was that he was a superficial fool to begin with. He considered it shameful to be reprimanded. He was ignorant of the example of Emperor Yao, who solicited advice from his subjects and sought out the opinion of a humble woodcutter. Nor did he appreciate why the Duke of Zhou went in person to receive low-ranking officials and General Han Xin begged his captured adversary Li Zuoche for advice on military strategy.[2] If even an emperor, king, or high minister would be modest enough to attend to the counsel of their subordinates, how could someone like Zhang reject a man's good advice just because of his low status? What a pity that Zhang was such an immature boy. Ignorant of past and present alike, he lacked the discernment to avoid being taken in by slander. Alas!

Notes

1. This would be after 1573, when the Wanli period began.
2. Yao was a sage ruler of early antiquity; the Duke of Zhou was a conscientious regent early in the Western Zhou (ca. 1045–771 B.C.E.); Han Xin (ca. 230–196 B.C.E.) assisted in the founding of the Han dynasty.

Type 8
Showing Off Wealth

Impersonating the Son of an Official to Steal a Merchant's Silver

Chen Dong, from Shandong province, had for many years traveled to a place called Long Dike in Jianyang, Fujian, to trade in woven cloth. In spring of the thirty-second year of the Wanli period [1604], he traveled with two servants and over one thousand ounces of silver on his second cloth-buying trip to Long Dike. During the journey, a crook secretly observed that Chen was carrying a lot of money. Though he coveted his money, the crook could also see that Chen was a seasoned veteran of the trade who always set out late, retired early, and closely guarded his property. An opening would be hard to find, so the crook took to impersonating a son of the General Surveillance Intendant for the Jiannan circuit. He played the part to the fullest, adopting the appropriate demeanor and bringing four servants to wait on him. At every stop he stayed at the same inn as Chen but didn't engage him in conversation. Nor did Chen pay him any mind.

They reached Qianshan county in Jiangxi province, whose vice magistrate, Cai Yuan, was from Guangdong province.[1] Cai and the circuit intendant were from different counties and did not know each other personally, so the disguised crook paid Cai a courtesy call. Hearing that it was the son of the circuit intendant, the vice magistrate received him courteously. He then paid a return visit, giving him money for traveling expenses. Chen, seeing the vice magistrate repay the courtesy call, believed that the crook really was the offspring of an official. That night, the crook invited Chen to join him for a banquet, which the crook paid for using the money he'd received from the Qianshan vice magistrate. Chen accepted with delight. Even so, he remained vigilant about being robbed and dared not drink too much. The crook still couldn't make his move.

The next day they stopped for the night in the small river port of Wushi. Chen was eager to reciprocate by hosting a banquet of his own, but he was unable to acquire the necessary provisions and had to give up on the idea. The following day they stopped for the night in Chong'an county.

We're getting close to Long Dike and I had better repay him, Chen thought, *especially considering his important lineage. Not to mention that he and I will be soon be parting, and it would be extremely impolite not to return the courtesy he's shown me.* He proceeded to purchase prepared dishes and invite the man to join him for a meal.

The crook said to Chen, "We crossed the Yangzi on the same boat and traveled all this way together. Clearly, we were destined to be companions. Tomorrow we go our separate ways. Who knows when we'll meet again?"

Both of them drank to their hearts' content. By the third watch, Chen's servants had all fallen fast asleep from exhaustion and he himself, sloshed, slumped over the table and fell asleep. The crook then stole all of Chen's property and fled.

When Chen awoke, the crook was nowhere to be found, so he went to the Chong'an county office and sued the innkeeper for conspiring against him. He then traveled to Guangxin prefecture and sued the vice magistrate for having collaborated with a crook, calling in the original innkeeper as a witness. The vice magistrate retorted, "To tell the truth, the Jiannan circuit intendant and I are from the same prefecture but different counties. I knew his surname but had never actually met his son. When he came to pay me a courtesy call and gave his surname, how could I, a lowly county magistrate, not return the courtesy or offer a parting gift? Chong'an is several days' journey from here. If he stole your silver, what does that have to do with me?"

Chen replied, "That crook followed the same itinerary as me all the way here, and I was vigilant in keeping him at bay. Only after he paid you a courtesy call and you returned his visit did I become convinced that he really was the son of an official and fall into his trap. He's an acquaintance of yours, so of course I'm going to bring you to court."

The prefect could not reach a verdict, so Chen took his case to the office of the Grand Surveillance Intendant, Venerable Shi. Shi ruled that the vice magistrate had erred in paying respects to the phony son of an official and in giving gifts away so lightly, misleading a traveling merchant in the process. Since all of this resulted from a public official's mistake, he awarded Chen one hundred ounces of silver in traveling expenses and sent him home.

Alas! This crook's scheme was ingenious! He impersonated the son of an official for the entire journey, but the merchant was wise enough to keep his guard up. But when he paid a courtesy call to the vice magistrate and the latter reciprocated, giving him a parting gift—who would have doubted that he really was from such a family? He laid another trap by inviting the merchant to drink with him, so that the merchant would, as a matter of course, repay the courtesy. In obliging the merchant to drink with him, he befuddled host and servants alike and had no trouble pulling off his nighttime theft. That's why I say this scheme couldn't have been planned more brilliantly. Had Chen kept his guard up for just one more night, the crook's duplicity would have been for naught. It's true: initial vigilance is no substitute for constant vigilance. One can't let one's guard down day or night. Doing so would be like carrying a jug to fetch water and smashing it just as you reach the well—the same type of carelessness. I hope that merchants can learn to be as scrupulous in concluding their undertakings as they are in beginning them!

Note

1. A vice magistrate (here, *xiancheng* 縣丞) was a second-in-command appointed to manage particularly populous, strategic, or difficult-to-govern counties. Local histories of Qianshan, located in Guangxin prefecture, Jiangxi province, list all the holders of this office, and the name Cai Yuan does not appear among them.

Flashy Clothing Incites Larceny

You Tiansheng, from Huizhou prefecture, was a man of splendid appearance and imposing elegance; he was also something of a clotheshorse. One day he set off to buy iron in Jianning prefecture, taking along his servant Xu Ding and capital of more than five hundred ounces of silver. Reaching Chong'an county, he boarded a riverboat[1] captained by a man named Li Ya, who was assisted by a deckhand named Weng Yah.[2] This Li Ya had earlier bankrupted his family with his whoring and gambling, then turned to skippering a boat as a last resort.

When the boat reached Jianyang county, Tiansheng, in preparing to disembark to visit a relative in the vicinity, opened his trunk and took out a striking robe. Li Ya saw that the trunk was filled with exquisite outfits, and the sight of this gave him a notion. That evening, when Tiansheng asked the captain to buy him some wine and a meal, Li slipped some *tuotuo* blossoms into the wine. (*Tuotuo* flowers are also known as datura; whoever consumes them becomes comatose and unable to speak.)³ That night Tiansheng and his servant both succumbed to the drug and fell into a stupor. At midnight, Li tried to bring his deckhand in on the plot, but Weng Yah told him, "Wealth is allotted by fate, and it's wrong to chase after what's not yours. If word got out, there'd be no beating that rap. Count me out."

Li's rapaciousness would not be stopped by his deckhand's objections, and he tossed both passengers overboard into the depths. Tiansheng drowned, but his servant Xu Ding had luckily drunk less wine than his master, so the water revived him. An adept swimmer, he was able to make it to shore.

The next day, Xu Ding took a different boat to the Jianning prefectural seat. There he submitted a complaint to Prefect Wang, who promptly dispatched a search party of six soldiers to accompany Xu to Linjiang Junction to apprehend the suspect. (Linjiang Junction is a port where boats on their way to and from Jianning assemble.) They arrived to find Li Ya with the loot in his possession. He'd just bought some wine and was bringing it on board his boat, his mind fixed on revelry. Xu Ding pointed Li out to the soldiers, who locked him in shackles. They searched the boat for the stolen property and, finding it on board, brought the prisoner and the goods back to the prefectural seat.

As soon as Prefect Wang began his interrogation, Li Ya saw that the game was up. Unable to deny the charges, he gave a complete confession in which he implicated his deckhand as an accomplice.

Xu Ding testified, "When I was drugged, I was in a stupor and unable to speak, but in my dreamlike state I heard the deckhand urge him to stop. The deckhand didn't go along with the plot and fled before it was carried out. If you punish the man unjustly, it will dissuade others from doing the right thing in the future."

Prefect Wang sentenced Li Ya to forty blows, followed by imprisonment and decapitation, as prescribed by the statutes. Two guards accompanied Xu Ding back to You Tiansheng's home, along with Tiansheng's belongings and money. Li Ya's death sentence was carried out the following winter.

Later, Weng Yah gave up boating for agriculture, in which he prospered. Li Ya, in plotting against others, hastened his own death; by remonstrating against evil, Weng Yah was able to protect his family. True indeed is the saying: "Goodness brings good rewards, and evil brings evil rewards!"

You Tiansheng brought this disaster upon himself with his opulent attire, which made the thieving captain covetous. In general, when traveling alone by boat it is imperative to guard against the nefarious plots of boatmen. Nap during the day so that you'll be easily roused at night. When cooking meals and heating wine, be especially careful of people slipping you poison. Keep your dress modest and avoid anything flashy. Laozi said, "A good merchant hides things away and appears to have nothing," and Confucius said, "Few go astray who comport themselves with restraint."[4] *Wise words indeed for cultivating virtue and keeping harm at bay.*

Notes

1. Reading *qingliu* 清流 ("clear flow") for the homophone 青流 ("green flow"). According to Song Yingxing 宋應星 (1587–1666), the former was a name for shallow-draft vessels that transported goods and passengers between Chong'an and Fuzhou. Song, *Tiangong kaiwu* 天工開物 (1637 woodblock ed.), 2.36a.

2. The two personal names are homonyms except for tone, so we distinguish the latter as Yah.

3. *Tuotuo* flowers are used for the same purpose in the story "A Fake Scion Rents Rooms and Robs a Widow" (see appendix 2).

4. The quotations appear in the *Records of the Grand Historian* and *Analects.* See Sima Qian 司馬遷, *Shiji* 史記 (Beijing: Zhonghua shuju, 1982), 63.2141, and *Lunyu*, 4.23. Latter translation adapted from Edward G. Slingerland, *Confucius Analects: With Selection from Traditional Commentaries* (Indianapolis: Hackett, 2003), 37.

Type 9
Scheming for Wealth

Stealing a Business Partner's Riches
Only to Lose One's Own

Zhang Pei was a wealthy trader from Xiuning county in Huizhou prefecture whose capital ran into the thousands of ounces of silver. He once traveled to Guazhou to purchase three hundred-odd bales of raw cotton.[1] Liu Xing was a destitute, orphaned commoner from She county in Huizhou. Ten years earlier Liu had left home with a pack on his back to be a trader, but in the course of that time he had only scraped together seventy ounces of capital, which he had brought to the same shop as Zhang to buy cotton. The two were from different counties in the same prefecture, so once Zhang realized that Liu spoke the same dialect and they shared a similar temperament, they became as close as brothers. Having finished buying their cotton, they traveled together to the capital of Fujian province, both intending to sell it at the shop of the broker Chen the Fourth, where they also shared lodgings.

Within a few days, Liu had sold all his cotton. Zhang, meanwhile, had made more than five hundred ounces of silver from selling less than half his cotton. The sight of all that money gave Liu an evil notion. This he shared with a certain Zhao Tong, an unattached fellow who lived next door to the shop: "There's a trader in the shop who's got a lot of silver on him. Go to the southern docks to hire a rowboat and wait for me there. I'll bring the money, then we'll travel until we find a temple in the mountains to serve as our hideout. We'll split the loot fifty-fifty." Zhao agreed.

Liu then lied to Zhang, saying "A relative from back home and I were going to head to Haicheng to buy some imported goods from the south, but he hasn't shown up yet, so I have to wait a few more days."[2]

Then one day, when a business partner had asked Zhang to lunch, Liu bored a hole in the wall of their lodgings and removed the five hundred-plus ounces of silver from Zhang's trunk. He secreted it into his own crates and bundles, then hired someone to come to Chen the Fourth's and say that his relative had arrived and was asking him to head out right away.

Liu lied: "My luggage is all ready, but Brother Zhang went out for a drink and I haven't had a chance to say good-bye to him."

Zhang Pei's servant said, "Since my master's out at the moment, I'll pass along your respects."

Liu then said farewell to the shop owner Chen the Fourth. Being an experienced broker, Chen went to inspect Liu's quarters, but the hole that Liu had bored in the wall had been covered over. Liu hired porters to take his cargo to the seaport, but changed course en route and paid them to go to the southern docks, where he boarded the rowboat and went upriver toward the junction.

When Zhang returned, Chen the Fourth told him, "Your Huizhou compatriot has departed, and he asked that I send your honor his best wishes."

Zhang opened the door to his room and started at the sight of the gash cut into his trunk. "For crying out loud!" He opened it up and saw that all the silver had been stolen. A search turned up nothing. Chen the Fourth went to reinspect Liu's room and discovered the borehole in the wall. "What's done is done, and there's nothing we can do for the time being," he said. "But you and your servant should hire four runners to go straight to Haicheng. I'll get an official and round up seven or eight others to hire a rowboat to follow them to the junction."

So Chen went upriver in pursuit, and late that afternoon they met a boat coming downriver. He called out, "On your way down, did you see a boat with three people and three packs going upstream in a hurry?"[3]

The oarsman replied, "We did see three people disembarking with three packs at the junction."

Chen's boat arrived at the junction as dusk was falling, and no one was to be seen. Then they spotted two boys heading home with their oxen, and asked, "Three men carrying three packs passed by here a while ago—did you boys see them?"

The herdboys replied, "They were heading up toward the waterfall."

"Is there a village near there?"

"No, just a temple, called Highfalls Temple."

Chen the Fourth paid one of the boys a twentieth of an ounce of silver to show them the way to the temple. When they got there it was almost the third watch of the night. Chen said, "If we call for the temple gates to be opened, they're sure to flee. Let's split into two groups, one at the front gate and one guarding the back. Come morning, the monks will open the gates, and we can rush in before they have a chance to escape. We'll get 'em that way." "Good idea," the others agreed.

As soon as the monks opened the gate the next morning, the search party rushed in. "Where did you come from, gentlemen?" asked one of the stunned monks. Chen the Fourth explained their purpose, and asked when the three men had arrived at the temple. The monk replied, "They arrived after dark and are sleeping in that pavilion. They told us they had come here seeking refuge." He led the party in to arrest the three.

When they searched their captives they found that Zhang Pei's money was wrapped in one bundle while Liu's own seventy ounces were on his person, in a sack tied with a string. The three thieves prostrated themselves and pleaded for mercy. "I know I was wrong to take his silver, which I'll return," Liu said. "But I beg you to let me keep mine."

The pursuers ignored his pleas and pummeled the thieves half to death with rocks. Then they packed up the cargo, tied up the perpetrators, and escorted them back to Chen's shop. At the time, Zhang had not yet returned from Haicheng, but thousands of people, both visiting merchants and locals, gathered to watch their arrival. Liu was mortified and despondent. A few days later, when Zhang returned, he berated Liu: "You thief! You made me go all the way to Haicheng and back. It's a lucky thing for both of us that my silver's all here—I'll let you off this time. But from now on I want you to turn over a new leaf. If you ever act like this again, I'll see that you feel the full force of the law."

"There's a word you're forgetting," Liu said, "'hometown.'"

"Talk of 'hometown' is exactly what misled me," Zhang rejoined. "It's because of our previous friendship that I'm letting you off. Go on, get out of here."

"Let me have my silver back, I beg of you."

Liu's silver had already been seized by the crowd, so Zhang asked them to return it, saying he would make it up to them.

The crowd protested, "If this thief were to be tried in court, he probably wouldn't get away with his life. And now you're letting him off, and even letting him scrounge off you?"

They were about to lay into Liu Xing again when Zhang stopped them. "Your own unscrupulousness led you to commit this act," he told Liu, "and now it's come back to bite you—that's nothing to wring your hands about. But I'm going to be generous and give you five ounces of silver to get by on." Liu, moved to tears, scurried off.

Alas! Encountering a hometown acquaintance abroad is like sweet rain after a long drought. A traveler who meets a man from his hometown is wont to form a close fraternal bond with him and to wish to spend their days together. This is only human. It was inevitable that Zhang Pei and Liu Xing would share quarters, since they were in the same line of business and from the same place. How then could Liu harbor such nefarious intent, attacking from within the same house, coveting and stealing

Zhang's wealth! When he stole away on a rowboat, he told himself that his plan had worked. Little did he know that Heavenly justice will not countenance such treacherous thievery. So he ended up captured, beaten, and humiliated; overnight he lost the seventy ounces of silver he'd worked for decades to amass. He plotted for unearned gains and ended up losing his own earnings. What a fool! I was astounded by this story and record it to warn those with similar inclinations toward trickery or avarice. At the same time, this story reminds traders to be wary of duplicitous hometown thieves.

Notes

1. Guazhou was a commercial town at the juncture of the Grand Canal and the Yangzi River.
2. Haicheng was a seaport in Zhangzhou prefecture in southern Fujian province.
3. How could Chen have known that he was after *three* people? Presumably the pursuing party had acquired this information in the course of their inquiries.

Haughtiness Leads to a Lawsuit That Harms Wealth and Health

Wei Bangcai was a traveling merchant from Guangdong. He was the richest man in the whole province and extraordinarily arrogant, always crowing about his wealth. When he traveled on business he felt that no one was worthy of his regard.

Once he bought a hundred crates of silk thread in Huzhou and was on his way home to sell it in Guangdong. At Hangzhou he booked passage on a ship that was carrying twenty-some other merchants. While they were held up at Fuyang for most of a week because of high winds, his servants would get up early and fight to be the first to cook breakfast, while he would wander the ship starting arguments over any tiny thing that was not to his liking.[1] The other passengers, seeing how snooty Wei was and reckoning that they wouldn't have to spend too much time in his company, just let him have his way.

Wei's servants had taken on their master's disposition and also antagonized other passengers on a daily basis. Had Wei kept his servants in check and appeased his peers, all would have been well. But instead he would take their side and say offensive things like, "You vulgar riff-raff, not one of you is my equal!" He also kept going on about his enormous wealth, claiming, "I could personally buy all the cargo on this ship."

Having listened to such talk one too many times, the other passengers got fed up. As they were grumbling, a certain Wang Fengqi, who came from a prominent Huizhou lineage with a long tradition of office holding, expressed indignation at how Wei was using his wealth to lord it over everyone. "You're constantly talking about your thousands in gold, but life is long and things change. Once upon a time, Shi Chong was even richer than you, but what did that get him in the end?"[2]

Wei, incensed at this attack, shot back, "You're all scum—every one of you! If there's a man of substance on board this boat, I haven't heard a peep from him yet. Go ahead and show me what you've got—see if you can match a hundred crates of silk thread worth thousands in gold."

"Vulgar wretch!" Wang replied disparagingly. "Your lack of taste is matched only by your willful insolence. You're finished and you don't even know it, loser. My fortune easily trumps yours, and I'll send you home in a box!"

Wei and Wang argued nonstop, and the other passengers were secretly excited to see them duke it out. Only after one of Wang's supporters had urged him to back down did everyone retire to their cabins.

The next day, a passenger named Li Hanqing went around telling people how fortunate he thought it was that they had Brother Wang to stand up to Wei. Overhearing this, Wei laid into Li and dragged Wang in as well, cursing them in the foulest of terms. The other passengers were indignant at Wei's insulting rant. "If this whole boatload of people is going to be bullied by one man, we should all take a blood oath against him."

"With your help," Wang offered, "I'm willing to take him on and slake your thirst for vengeance. He's got those hundred crates of silk. Help me beat him half to death, and he'll be sure to file a complaint; I'll then hide half of his silk somewhere else and leave him half for the court battle. Then we'll destroy his original account records. Now when he files charges against me, whatever you do, be sure to stand firm. When you testify on my behalf, we'll have to keep our stories straight. We'll let him sell off his silk until he's used it up—that's what they call 'Wishing him a Happy New Year while wearing the shirt you've taken off his back'! A court battle is a life-and-death struggle."

"Sounds good," the other passengers agreed. "All we want is to get back at him."

Making sure there would be no leaks, they finalized the plan. Wang then went several rounds with Wei on the deck of the boat, and the humiliated Wei ran off to file a complaint at the county office. Once the complaint had been accepted, Wang moved half of Wei's thread to a secret location and proceeded to destroy all of Wei's account records and all of the receipts for the taxes and duties he'd paid. His own goods he deposited in the shop of the broker Zhang Chun.

When Wei came back on board and found some of his thread missing, he started another fight with Wang. He then went to amend his complaint, adding that fifty crates of thread had been stolen, with the merchants on board and the captain as witnesses.

Wang Fengqi smeared pig's blood all over his head and had two people carry him into the yamen, reporting an attempt on his life. He gave a hundred ounces of silver to his maternal uncle Huo, who was from his hometown and was serving in the local administration. Wei Bangcai gave a hundred and fifty ounces to a local holder of the metropolitan *jinshi* degree, Wei Xian, and to nine holders of the provincial *juren* degree; Wang then gave another two hundred ounces to the same men. Wei Xian and the others had first contacted the magistrate on Wei Bangcai's behalf. But when they followed up shortly thereafter with letters that contradicted the earlier ones and supported Wang, the two submissions did not line up. Investigators began to take testimony, and the ship's captain said that it was true that there had been a fight but he hadn't seen any thread being removed. So when the magistrate ruled, he declared the matter of the thread uncertain and based his decision only on the assault charge, judging both parties to be partly responsible.

Dissatisfied with this outcome, Wei Bangcai appealed to the circuit court, where it was assigned to Judge Chen, who took depositions from, and was bribed by, both plaintiff and defendant. In the end, he upheld the original judgment from the county court. Wei tried to bump it up again to various higher civil and military agencies, and ultimately to the Ministry of Justice in Nanjing, but all of them affirmed the original verdict.

Over the course of the following year, as the two battled in court, Wei Bangcai used up all the proceeds from selling his thread and had to call in his brother for help. After he had burned through another five hundred ounces from his brother, he fell sick in his inn and an uncle was called in to check on him. This uncle was a loyal and kind family elder, and it was only after he had inquired into the backstory that he realized that it was his nephew's arrogance that had brought this upon him. The other merchants came forward to say they wanted an amicable resolution to the whole affair, and to wrap things up administratively each contributed a hundred ounces of silver, of which fifty would go to pay Wei's way home.

When Wei Bangcai got home, he thought back on his days as a merchant, on all the goods and money he'd moved from one place to another and how he had now returned empty-handed. Filled with wistful regret, he suffered mockery and insults from his family members, which only increased his stress. Within a few months he was afflicted with ulcers and died.

Alas! Wei Bangcai's wealth made him conceited, and he was spiteful and cruel to servants and neighbors alike. People let him have his way, but this only worsened his self-aggrandizing character and inflated his ego beyond all reason. As a result, when he went traveling on business he behaved like a narrow-minded fool—a frog who couldn't see beyond the well he lived in. His incessant boasting about his money showed that he was unable to think about anyone but himself. When he provoked Wang Fengqi and the rest into their plot of moving his silk and launching a lawsuit, he thought at first that he could simply deploy his wealth to dominate others with bribes. Wang and the others, to him, were mere playthings. When magistrates, prefects, judges, and the Ministry of Justice get involved, however, wealth is all for naught. At that point, he was a "ram stuck in a hedge"[3] who became sick with despair and full of regret. If not for his uncle's perspicuity in understanding the situation and extracting him from it, he might have died of despair far from home, becoming a ghost in a foreign land. Since antiquity it has been recorded that "the modest receive rewards and the self-satisfied invite ruin."[4] Hence the sages teach us again and again to treat ordinary people as one's betters and never to use state power to be domineering.[5] Pride has been the undoing of innumerable kings, dukes, and other great men— to say nothing of ordinary nobodies! Vanity is to be avoided even within the confines of the household—how much more so when in foreign parts! Merchants traveling far from home and hearth must strike a balance between being firm and being soft in their dealings with people from other regions. They must remain observant and prepared for unexpected adversity. Never can they afford to treat others disdainfully. Hence the saying, "Treat others amicably, and all will be your brothers within the four seas; be full of yourself, and you'll face a boatload of enemies."[6] Reflect upon this, merchants, and upon yourselves.

Notes

1. Fuyang was the first county inland from the seat of Hangzhou prefecture along the Qiantang River.
2. The famously rich and haughty Shi Chong was executed for refusing to cede his beautiful concubine Lüzhu to his ruler.
3. The image of a ram with its horns caught in a hedge, unable to move forward or back, comes from the statement on the third line of hexagram #34 (Dazhuang 大壯) in the *Book of Changes*.
4. These famous adages appear (in the reverse order) in the "Counsel of Yu the Great" (Dayu mo 大禹謨) in the *Book of Documents*.

5. The warning against being domineering on the basis of political power can be traced to a statement attributed to the Duke of Zhou in the *Records of the Grand Historian*. Sima Qian, *Shiji*, 33.1518.

6. The idea that "all men are brothers" is from the Confucian *Analects* 12.5 (albeit with a different set of conditions). The idea of fellow passengers being enemies appears in the *Records of the Grand Historian*. Sima Qian, *Shiji*, 65.2167.

Type 10

Robbery

Robbing a Pawnshop by Pretending to Leave Goods There

Beside a county yamen was a huge pawnshop that stocked tens of thousands of items and would accept anything that anyone brought, in whatever quantity. One day a customer of dignified appearance came in. He bowed politely as he entered, sent his people away, and said to the proprietor, "Let me be perfectly frank with you, sir. I come from another prefecture and have long been in the same line of work as you. Over the years I have accumulated a large stock of goods. Last month, I obtained from a corrupt official nine pole-crates[1] of precious goods. They happen to be stored in your fair county, and I find myself temporarily unable to sell them. If your establishment would be willing to take them on, I would ask to be paid one tenth of their estimated value in advance, then after the goods are sold to divide the proceeds at a rate of five hundred per thousand, payable in a year."

"I'd like to take a look at the goods," said the pawnbroker.

"There's a great quantity of things, nine pole-crates full, and it would be unwise to unpack them out in the open," answered the robber. "Tonight, tell the keeper of the city gate not to close up until we've concluded our business,[2] and hire eighteen men to meet my boat and carry the goods into the shop. Then we can inspect the goods, arrive at an estimate of their value, and make the exchange. I'll just take the prepayment now and collect the rest next year."

"Agreed."

That night, the pawnbroker told the gatekeeper to leave the gate open and hired eighteen porters to go to the riverbank to pick up the goods. They came back into the shop with the nine crates.

After the porters had left, the pawnbroker closed the doors to the outside. The robber unlocked the crates, then shouted, "Out, quick!" From each crate sprang two men armed with daggers. They tied up the pawnbroker with the warning, "Make a sound and you're dead."

The nineteen men forced their way into the house and tied up all the men and women. Then they emptied the store of its goods and loaded them into the crates, which they carried out through the city gates, telling the gatekeeper as they passed through, "You can lock up now." Then they sailed away in the dead of the night.

Later that night, one member of the family managed to loosen his bonds and untie the rest. They rushed to the city gate but found it locked. "Did you see anyone carrying pole-crates?" they asked the gatekeeper.

"The guys with the crates left hours ago," he replied.

At the fifth watch the gate was opened, but the robbers' boat had left during the night and there was no telling which way it had gone.

The man came to the store alone and the crates were all carried by hired porters, so it's no surprise that the pawnbroker didn't have his guard up. But even if there were nine full crateloads, why didn't he go himself to view them on the boat during the day? If he had inspected the goods then and there, the robber's scam would have been over before it began. By agreeing to a nighttime delivery and arranging for the city gate to be kept open, the pawnbroker succumbed to the plot, opening the door and welcoming the robbers. What a pity that "desire for profit makes even the wise foolish."

Notes

1. A container transported by hanging it at the center of a long pole, with one person carrying either end. The text here reads "seven pole-crates," which we have emended to nine to be consistent with the text that follows.
2. Cities were usually under curfew: the gates to the city wall were closed each night and not reopened until the next morning.

Type 11
Violence

Sticking a Plaster in the Eyes to Steal a Silver Ingot

In a county town there lived a silversmith whose family was extremely wealthy. He prospered in part because when revenue transporters collected the fall harvest tax they usually relied on him to cast the silver.

One day, after he had cast an ingot, he found a spot where the threads on the surface didn't show through. That night he set it in a boiling pot to clean it off.[1] The door of his shop had a big gap in it through which one could see in from the outside.

That very night, a crook who had bought a large medicinal plaster snuck over and spied on him. When the crook saw that the silversmith had finished washing the ingot and placed it beside his forge, he began to cry out as if in pain.

"Open up!"

"Who's there?"

"I've been beaten up by bandits! Please let me warm up this plaster on your forge so I can apply it to my wounds."

The silversmith opened the door and let him in. The crook gave every appearance of having a broken limb: his hands shook and he moaned in pain; his hair was disheveled and his head was bent. The crook took the plaster to the forge and heated up the side with the ointment. Then, holding the cloth backing in both hands, he pressed it onto the silversmith's face. In a trice, he snatched the ingot and fled. The silversmith, in unbearable pain, ripped off the scalding plaster and frantically wiped away the ointment. By then, however, the crook had vanished with the stolen ingot.

"Thief!" he cried, running out in pursuit. But he didn't know which way the crook had gone, and after running around in circles for a while he returned home, dejected.

This thief's ploy of feigning injury and yelling outside the door, then heating his ointment at the forge was a hard one to spot, to be sure. But an ingot is a valuable item, and one should guard against loss by storing it away before one opens the door. This story goes to show that if something seems peculiar about someone, one should be wary of letting them get close when one has silver in one's possession.

Note

1. A pattern of fine, concentric, ripple-like marks on the top of an ingot was a sign of its purity, so making these visible helped to ensure that the silver would pass muster in the marketplace.

Type 12

On Boats

Bringing Mirrors Aboard a Boat Invites a Nefarious Plot

Xiong Gao, of Zhangfu,[1] was the son of a prominent family. He was strong enough to subdue a tiger and proficient in the use of sticks and clubs. One night he was bringing two serving girls to the rear garden for a tryst when a tiger leaped in over a wall. They retreated into the house and came back out with an iron poker and large staves. The tiger charged from across the garden, but Xiong held it at bay with the poker. Forcing it to the ground with ease, he struck a quick blow. The tiger lurched forward again, and Xiong jabbed it once more with the poker. The tiger immediately turned tail to flee, but Xiong caught up with it and struck it such a blow from behind that it collapsed. "Help, quick!" he shouted, and the two serving girls ran up and bludgeoned the tiger to death with their staves. He was thenceforth known as "Xiong the Fourth, Tiger Killer."

Some time later he got a notion to take a tour of famous scenic spots and informed his elder brother, "I'm going leave the county to travel on business."

His brother tried to dissuade him: "You're such a straight-forward guy, don't even think of trying to make money. You're so naïve that I'm afraid you'd come to grief."

"Our old servant Man Qi is strong and wise. I should be fine if he comes along."

His brother was unable to deter him, and Xiong set off, taking with him more than a hundred ounces of silver. "I'm off to find opportunities to buy goods for trade," he announced. "Even if I don't make a profit, I doubt I'll lose my capital. No one can take advantage of me!"

He traveled from Zhejiang province south to Guangdong. When they came across goods worth buying, Man Qi would advise his master, "This is a good price. If we buy them and sell them back home we're sure to make a profit."

"I've come all this way and haven't seen the local sights yet," Xiong would reply. "If we buy goods now we'll be too laden down to travel freely."

Man Qi repeatedly urged Xiong to buy things, but each time Xiong ignored his servant's advice. Man Qi came to realize that his master's real goal was not money making but sightseeing. From then on, he let his master have his way, drinking when he drank and generally following his lead. Within half a year, they had exhausted two thirds of their capital.

"If we don't head back now we won't have anything left for traveling expenses," Man Qi reminded him.

Xiong replied, "We might not have much money left, but I still want to buy a few things to bring back as gifts from my journey."

After frittering away another two months, they arrived in Huzhou. Man Qi again urged him to start for home.

"What's good to buy here?" Xiong asked.

"The brushes and ink are excellent," Man Qi said.

"I'm not an expert and have no eye for those things—I'd probably get cheated. Shouldn't I buy something else for my mother, sister-in-law, and wife? The little money I have has to cover all of them."

"Then buy silks or mirrors," Man Qi suggested.

"I don't have enough for silk, and that's not my line either," Xiong said. "I'd be better off just buying them ten writing sets and ten mirrors."

"Fine."

They made the purchases in a hurry and headed home with just two small trunks.

"We got some great stuff," Xiong remarked, "and this way we can travel light."

They made their way to the riverside to board a boat. The captain observed that Xiong possessed the dignified bearing of a rich man and was attended by a well-turned-out servant. He found it odd, though, that his luggage consisted only of two small trunks. Carrying them on board, he discovered that they were extremely heavy and concluded that they must be filled with silver.

"Where do you hail from, sir?" he inquired, sizing Xiong up. "I'm surprised that you haven't bought more goods."

Xiong had little money on him and was worried that the other merchants on board would look down on him, so he lied: "I'm on my way home from Huguang province, where my brother is serving as an official. I haven't had a chance to buy anything."

"So you're from an official family," the captain replied.

Seeing that he had such a respectful and attentive servant who always addressed him as "Your Excellency," and that he was so open-handed, unlike the common run of merchants, the captain was even more convinced that he was dealing with a real relative of an official. Everyone on the boat treated him with respect and deference. When they reached the shore the other merchants all disembarked with their cargo. The captain detained just one passenger—Xiong—with an invitation: "During the crossing the boat was full of passengers and I didn't have a chance to pay my respects. I hope that Your Excellency will be willing to join me for a drink."

He then went ashore and bought a great array of prepared food and fine wine. That night the captain was a most attentive host and pressed wine on Xiong, who was in a good mood and drank heartily. The captain also spared no effort in encouraging his servant to drink. Man Qi could tell that the captain was up to no good, so he feigned putting up an initial resistance and then giving in to his entreaties to drink. After a few cups, he excused himself, saying that he was drunk and wanted to sleep. Xiong readily accepted the wine and really did end up dead to the world.

Man Qi, seeing his master sound asleep, got up and told the captain: "I'm not really drunk. We're so close to home now that I'm too depressed to drink. This young master is a wastrel who cares for nothing but wine and women. When his older brother was in office he gave him several hundred ounces of silver to be rid of him and sent him home. But my master whored away all of the money on the road. All he's bringing home are a few writing brushes and mirrors as gifts for his nephews. When the old master gets home tomorrow he's certain to blame me for having failed to restrain him. But how am I supposed to restrain a guy like this? He downs wine like it's syrup, and he's always bragging. Here, take a look in his luggage and you tell me if there's a scrap of silver in there."

He unlocked the two trunks and the captain saw that they contained no money at all, only writing brushes and mirrors. Qi took out two mirrors and presented them to the captain. "Thank you for taking such good care of us on this journey—here's one mirror from each of us."

"You shouldn't be giving away your master's things," the captain told him.

"You could take half of them and he wouldn't notice they were missing 'til he got home."

Man Qi locked up the trunks again, and both he and the captain turned in. Man Qi, however, kept watch through the night.

"The captain treated us so well on this trip," Xiong remarked as they were docking the next day. "Give him an extra tenth of an ounce of silver."

When they arrived home, Man Qi said, "Count the mirrors to see if any are missing."

Xiong counted them and noted, "Two are missing."

"I gave away those two mirrors to save our hides. Were you aware of that, Master?"

"What's this crazy talk?"

Man Qi gave a detailed account of what had happened when they were drinking on the boat. "Why would anyone lay out such an extravagant spread for someone who was about to leave, unless they were up to no good and trying to butter you up?"

Xiong was shocked. "You're right! If you hadn't been so shrewd, we'd have been goners!"

The family was delighted to learn of their close escape and rewarded Man Qi.

Xiong was born into an easy life and grew into a hedonist and brag-gart. He knew nothing of the perils of real life. If it hadn't been for Man Qi's astuteness, Xiong would have tossed their lives away, and they would be feeding the fishes. For a master who has to travel afar but lacks experience, a conscientious servant is an invaluable companion. Hence in "Traveling" the loss of a serving boy is treated as a calamity and finding a serving boy is a great boon: such is the great significance that the sages attached to "Traveling"![2]

Notes

1. There is no recorded place with the name Zhangfu 章富. This may be a miswriting of Zhangpu 漳浦, a locale in Fujian province, or the name may be intentionally fictive.
2. The closing of this comment references and draws its wording from hexagram #56 (Lü 旅, Traveling) in the *Book of Changes*.

Porters Run Off with Cargo from a Boat

When a boat arrives at the riverbank near Fuzhou porters mob it, hoping to be hired to carry a load into the city. An experienced merchant will shout at the swarm of porters to step back until all of his goods are unloaded onto the shore, checked, and fully accounted for. Only then will he divide them into bundles and call over a few porters he knows personally. When they finally set off into town, he'll have someone follow closely behind to ensure that nothing goes missing. When the arrival is a greenhorn, however, the porters don't care whether he's done inspecting and organizing his baggage—they'll just pack it into shoulder crates and take off. The owner is forced to give chase, often before all of his property is off the boat.

Once a certain *xiucai* surnamed Tian, from nearby Houguan county, had been away working as a tutor and was returning home at year end. He had with him forty ounces of silver he'd received as tuition payments as well as two large baskets of clothing, bedding, and other belongings worth another ten-odd ounces. Passing through Fuzhou, he wanted to pay his respects to a relative there, so he hired a porter to carry his baskets ahead of him. Tian, a Confucian scholar, followed with a leisurely gait. Seeing how slowly Tian moved, the porter picked up his pace. Rushing into the city gates, he darted into a crowded, bustling area at a breakneck pace before disappearing into the twisting alleyways. Tian chased him and shouted at the porter to stop, but to no avail. The alleys within the city walls snaked off in all directions and he had no chance of finding him.

The next day Tian went to the prefectural office and reported the porter to Constable Lü. Lü was a perspicacious officer. *If a porter has stolen the goods*, he figured, *it will take a porter to track him down*. He called in two runners and told them, "Take a good look at this Master Tian. This afternoon he will be wearing a white jacket and will arrive on a boat with some baggage, which some porter is sure to run off with. I want you two to tail him back to his place and then bring him here."

He then addressed Tian. "Make up a bundle of fake luggage and board a boat ten *li* from here later today. When you land, hire a porter to carry your luggage just like yesterday. Wear a white jacket so these two runners can spot you easily, and once the runners are nearby, make sure to walk slowly so that the porter will run away. That way we're sure to nab the guy."

Tian got the plan, and that afternoon he arrived on a boat that he'd boarded with his fake luggage ten *li* upstream. Once he and the runners had spotted each other, he called for a porter to take his bags, and sure enough, when he slowed his steps, the porter ran off. The runners tailed the porter to his house, where they apprehended him, saying, "Venerable Lü wants to see you."

The porter, Huang the Third, had no clue what had happened, and all he could do was go along with them. Lü asked him, "What were you doing carrying off a *xiucai*'s baggage?"

"I was just taking it to my place for a little while, but I intended to return it," replied the distressed porter.

The officer had just ordered five blows for Huang when Tian came in. "Today," Lü told Huang, "I'm giving you a chance to atone for your crime. Yesterday, a porter ran off with this gentleman's belongings. I'm giving you two days to find him; if you don't, know that you'll pay for it."

"We work at the river on alternate days," Huang said. "Yesterday it wasn't my shift."

"Then you'll just have to track down whoever it was."

Huang spent two fruitless days searching. On the third day, as the runners were bringing him in, he noticed another porter, Liu the Fifth, exchanging three tenths of an ounce of silver for coins and then using the money to buy fish and meat. Hauled into court again, Huang could only offer this: "I didn't find anything, but just now I did see Liu the Fifth changing money and buying a lot of fish and meat, which is suspicious."

The constable immediately dispatched four men, along with Tian and Huang the Third, to search Liu's place. In the cramped quarters they found both him and the loot. Brought to the yamen, Liu confessed: "The money and the stuff are all there. For the past five days I haven't dared to step out the door. Only today did I venture out to exchange just three tenths of an ounce of silver for coins, so I could buy myself a little something. It's true, I stole it."

The constable ordered twenty blows for Liu on the spot, and said, "Both of you stole from clients, so you'll both be sentenced to penal servitude. But, Huang the Third, you redressed your crime by assisting in the capture of Liu the Fifth. I'll let you go with another ten blows as a warning. Liu the Fifth, I will take your poverty into account and let you go when everything is paid back."

Constable Lü called Tian back in to sign for receipt of his recovered property. In just a few days Lü had caught the criminal—a feat possible only for a true administrative genius!

Porters running off with people's goods happens everywhere, so be extremely mindful of this when traveling. Constable Lü identified the wrongdoer only because he spared no effort to capture the thief. Success came thanks to his move of finding one porter with another, a strategy akin to "attacking barbarians with barbarians." This is the same as the old adage, "A thief catches a thief as a needle pricks a thorn." This story offers a warning to those who hire porters and a method for those who would catch thieves.

Type 13

Poetry

Swindling the Salt Commissioner While Disguised as Daoists

Tang Yin had two style names, Bohu and Ziwei, and was from the neighborhood of Wuqu in Nanjing. He placed first in the provincial examination of 1498 but was dismissed due to a scandal and thereafter traveled around leading an unrestrained life, dallying with wine and courtesans. He excelled at both poetry and prose, and was an accomplished painter as well. His friends included Wen Zhengming, Wen Zhengzhong, and Zhu Yunming—all leading lights of the day.[1] Every day they roved the pleasure quarters of Nanjing, entertaining themselves by matching wits and composing literary pieces off the cuff.

Once a subaltern clerk came by with a sheet of paper to request a painting. Tang Yin picked up a brush and drew ten-odd snails, then added a colophon:

Forget swimming crabs and razor clams,
true delicacies of the seas are these!

Holler ten thousand times—he's snug in his shack
'til someone gives his butt a smack.

Everyone laughed aloud.[2]

Another day Tang went out and happened to see a monk in a cangue before the county offices. "Could you write a poem for this monk?" someone in the crowd asked. Tang Yin inquired as to why the monk was there, then picked up a brush and wrote on the cangue around the monk's neck,

A clerk sent out to tax the tea
sought silver as a bribe, did he.
When thirty blows in court were reaped,
on this square plate a melon heaped.[3]

The magistrate, leaving his office to send off a visitor, spotted the poem and asked who had written it. When someone told him it was Tang Yin, the magistrate set the monk free. Such was his quick wit.

On one occasion, Tang Yin, Zhu Yunming, and a dozen or so of their comrades packed their bags and went off to Yangzhou. They spent their days drinking with courtesans, lost in debauchery. Within a month their spending money began to run out.

"We're out of cash—what's the plan?" Zhu asked.

"No problem!" Tang replied. "The salt commissioner is loaded. The two of us can disguise ourselves as Daoist priests from the Temple of the Lady's Purity to 'transform' him." So they dressed up as Daoists and made their way to the salt commissioner.

Entering the hall, they prostrated themselves at the foot of the stairs. "Daoists of the Temple of the Lady's Purity requesting an audience!"

The salt commissioner was furious. "Are you unaware of the frosty winds blowing in from the censorate?[4] You've got gall! What Dao led you to approach me in such an improper manner?"

He was on the point of thrashing them when they calmly replied, "Do you imagine, my lord, that we wandered here in search of food? We Daoists have traveled throughout the realm, socializing with only its most famous personages. In Suzhou, for example, none other than Tang Yin, Wen Zhengming, and Zhu Yunming have been so kind as to befriend us, since on the spur of the moment we can invent any manner of poem, lyric, song, or rhapsody. Should your lordship doubt our humble skills, might we present a little something in response to your command?"

The salt commissioner pointed to the stone ox at the entrance to the hall and commanded the pair to compose matching couplets on that theme. Tang Yin responded immediately by intoning the line,

> An odd stone leans on the clouds of a lofty peak.

Zhu Yunming continued,

> How many years has it lain abandoned there?

Tang: Its coat of shaggy moss grows in the rain;
Zhu: the vines that pierce its nose dangle in the wind.
Tang: Never has it eaten creekside grass,
Zhu: nor ever plowed the bordered fields.
Tang: Strangely silenced, the herdboy stays his whip,
Zhu: yet a note from his flute hangs on moonlit smoke.

When the salt commissioner had taken this in, he said in a mollified tone, "Fine verse indeed! What is it you wish to do?"

"Of late," they answered, "the Temple of the Lady's Purity has fallen into disrepair. We heard that your lordship is a generous man and fond of good works, so we hope that you might make a contribution to support the renovation of the temple. This would be of everlasting benefit."

The salt commissioner was delighted and immediately wrote to the Vice Magistrate of Wuxing, authorizing him to withdraw five hundred ounces of silver from the treasury.[5] When Tang and Zhu saw that the salt commissioner had agreed to their request, they traveled overnight to Wuxing, where, pretending to speak on behalf of the Daoists, they discussed the transaction with the vice magistrate: "An envoy from the salt commissioner will be here shortly, requesting funds to repair the Temple of the Lady's Purity. You should provide everything he asks for and not stint in the least."

The vice magistrate gave them the full amount. Tang and Zhu were delighted when they received the money, and exclaimed, "You can't snatch the pearl from under the dragon's neck unless you plumb the depths of the pool!"

Then they returned to Yangzhou, where they joined their ten-odd comrades disporting themselves in the pleasure quarters, organizing opera performances, drinking, and reveling in every pleasure. In less than twenty days all of the silver had been spent.

Meanwhile, the salt commissioner went to Wuxing on an inspection tour. He donned his robe and cap and visited the Temple of the Lady's Purity, which he found to be just as dilapidated as before. He summoned the vice magistrate and berated him.

The vice magistrate responded, "A few days ago, Tang Yin and Zhu Yunming came from Yangzhou, full of praise for your lordship for undertaking this great act. So your humble servant provided exactly what was asked."

Although the salt commissioner felt miserable when he realized that Tang and Zhu had swindled him, he admired their rare talent and let the matter rest.[6]

Tang Yin and Zhu Yunming were two of the most illustrious men of their time, but failing to achieve their ambitions they turned to worldly pleasures and their names were heard in every brothel and tavern. Were it not for their flowing eloquence and dashing talent, how could they have shaken up (and down) the state offices? This deserves to be called a good swindle in every sense of the word. Just consider the leading talents and influential scholars of our day, all of whom think only of squeezing commoners to fill their own purses and exploit popular grievances solely to enrich their own families—how they swindle the common people! For one of them to be swindled in turn by Tang and Zhu serves as a warning to the corrupt. Still, the salt commissioner's choice not to pursue the matter after realizing what had happened shows a certain sympathy for men of talent.

Notes

1. The author here betrays his ignorance of recent history: Wen Zhengming 文徵明 and Wen Zhengzhong 文徵仲 are alternate names for the same person, Wen Bi 文壁 (1470–1559). Tang Yin and Zhu Yunming 祝允明 (1461–1527) are also historical personages. All three were famous as writers, painters, and calligraphers; Wen and Zhu were also successful scholar-officials. Tang Yin, who rose to cultural prominence from a humble merchant background but experienced frustration in his official career, was the subject of extensive popular lore, of which this story is an example.

2. A slightly different version of this anecdote appears in a collection of biographical sketches of Tang Yin appended to a collection of his works published in 1614. It seems likely that Zhang Yingyu adapted his version, along with that of the main story in this entry, from that collection. See Tang Yin 唐寅, *Tang Bohu xiansheng quanji* 唐伯虎先生全集, photoreproduction of 1614 Nanya tang ed. (Taipei: Xuesheng shuju, 1970), *waibian* 3.10a.

3. Presumably, the clerk was collecting both taxes and kickbacks from a monastic tea plantation and punished a monk who failed to pay him off.

4. The censorate was a powerful branch of the Ming government that kept tabs on the activities of all officials and punished corruption and other malfeasance.

5. Taking the otherwise unattested title *erxian* 二縣 as meaning "second in command in the county," following the model of *erfu* 二府, a standard term for a vice prefect. Wuxing is an informal designation for Huzhou in northern Zhejiang.

6. Like the first anecdote about the clerk, this story appears, with significant variation, among the biographical sketches appended to Tang Yin's works. One version has been translated by T. C. Lai. See Tang Yin, *Tang Bohu xiansheng quanji*, *waibian*, 7a–8a, and T. C. Lai, *T'ang Yin, Poet/painter, 1470–1524* (Hong Kong: Kelly and Walsh, 1971), 105–6. He Dacheng 何大成 (fl. 1614), the editor of the collection, cites a very similar poem by the early Ming poet Gao Qi 高啓 (1336–1374); cf. Gao Qi, *Daquan ji* 大全集, in *Wenyuan ge Siku quanshu* 文淵閣四庫全書, 15.35a. The modern editor of Tang's works considers both the poem and the anecdote spurious. See Zheng Qian 鄭騫, ed., *Tang Bohu shi jiyi jianzhu* 唐伯虎詩輯逸箋注 (Taipei: Lianjing, 1982), 168–69.

7. See note 13 in the introduction on the historical Chen Quan.

8. Reading *pei* 賠 as *pei* 陪.

Chen Quan Scams His Way Into the Arms of a Famous Courtesan

Chen Quan was a suave and debonair millionaire from Nanjing.[1] He was also a wag who could instantly come up with a pithy rhyme for any new thing or situation. Although he was a habitué of the city's brothels, only one prostitute truly struck his fancy.

One summer, just as melons were coming into season, someone from that prostitute's brothel, as a practical joke, hid two melon peels just inside the threshold of the front door and then sent a messenger running to Chen in a panic: "Sister So-and-So is dying of a sudden illness and is saying she wants to see you one more time before she closes her eyes forever."

Chen leaped on his horse and galloped right over. As he rushed through the gate, his foot landed on the melon peels and he was sent sprawling. All the prostitutes clapped their hands in delight and burst out laughing. "Quick, Master Chen—a poem!"

Chen replied with:

Chen Quan, too quick to his heels,
fell for a brothel trap long laid;
and on account of two loose peels
with his life he almost paid.

The courtesans were delighted and had him stay for a drink.

Yet another day, he went boating with the ladies, who, when they came across a newly made boat, urged him, "Grace it with a verse—quick, now!"

In a trice, Chen came out with:

A craft as new as new can be,
blushing lotus in the pond was she.
Now become but a mere ferry,
obliging thousands, for a fee.
Have money? Climb on for a ride.
No dough? You'll be tossed aside.
Taken for a bath, drained, not dried,
yet—reach the other shore and you'll call for more!

The courtesans all sighed with delight and admiration.

Chen Quan's amusing verses were all of this sort.

Around that time, there was a renowned Hangzhou courtesan known as Peerless Blossom. She carried herself with exquisite deportment and was skilled in all the refined arts—the zither, chess, poetry, and painting. Her price, however, was exorbitant. She disdained to consort with the common herd and would receive only superior clients. A single night with her would set you back no less than six or seven ounces of silver.

Chen wanted this courtesan as soon as he heard of her, so he came up with a ruse. He ordered a dozen-odd family servants to transport a succession of boats to Hangzhou, and then traveled there himself with two or three other domestics. When he arrived at Peerless Blossom's place, he ordered his servants to use carrying poles to bring in a leather-covered chest. The bottom layers consisted entirely of paper-wrapped bricks, while the paper on the top layer all enclosed real silver, ten ounces to a package. Entering Peerless Blossom's bedroom, they opened the chest in front of her and distributed generous gifts of silver to the various servants. To Peerless Blossom herself Chen presented ten ounces of the finest silver. Peerless and her servants were delighted, believing Chen to be a man of considerable substance and foreseeing a potential windfall.

"May I know where you hail from, sir?" Peerless asked.

"Nanjing," Chen replied.

"May I ask your honorable surname?"

"Rake."

"And your poetic name?"

"Winning."

Peerless Blossom entertained her visitor with a lavish banquet, and "Winning Rake" thereupon took up residence in her chambers. After two days passed, another of his servants arrived to report that such-and-such a boat had arrived. Rake instructed, "Keep the cargo in the boat, but carry the leather case up here and put it in Miss Blossom's place."

This happened three or four times, and five or six leather cases accumulated in Peerless Blossom's bedroom. Rake, seeing that Blossom wore pearls, remarked, "Those pearls of yours are no good. I own several hundred large pearls, each perfectly round. When that boat arrives, I'll give them to you."

After about a month or so, the self-styled Winning Rake felt sated. When another servant arrived to say that such-and-such a boat had arrived, Rake said to Blossom, "This boat's cargo is different from the earlier ones. It's extremely valuable, and I'll have to go check on it in person. While I'm there, I'll pick up those pearls for you. I'll need you to take care of these cases of mine, which we'll keep safe in your bedroom. I won't be back until afternoon, so I'll trouble you to lend me a mount and send one of your servants to accompany me."

Peerless Blossom ordered a servant to attend him, and the servant set off with Rake on a donkey. Halfway there, Rake exclaimed, flustered, "I forgot my key! I stored it in your mistress's bedroom and forgot to bring it with me when I set off. Go back and get it for me."

"Hold on," the servant rejoined. "I'll need a note in your handwriting before she'll entrust me with your key. I won't be able to get it otherwise."

Rake dismounted from the donkey and went into a stationery store, where he wrote down the following couplets:

> Peerless Blossom of Hangzhou
> a wealthy Rake did come to know.
> She sent a man with an ass in tow,
> but off they went and those pearls won't show.[2]

He sealed the paper up and sent it back with the servant. As soon as Peerless Blossom read this missive she knew she'd been tricked. She hurriedly opened the crates to discover that they were filled with bricks. Rake had made advance arrangements for a servant to buy him passage on a waiting boat, and as soon as he reached the river they sailed back to Nanjing. Although Peerless Blossom would later make inquiries and discover that the perpetrator was none other than Chen Quan of Nanjing, by that time there was nothing to be done.

Courtesans swindle people by habit. Get off lightly and you'll lose only your fortune; get in deep and you'll lose your life. This is the first courtesan I've ever heard of who was herself swindled. And it was none other than Peerless Blossom, who had hiked her price sky high and defrauded countless would-be patrons out of a fortune. Little did she imagine that someone like Chen Quan would cook up such a diabolical scheme, and the man she sent with a donkey to keep tabs on him was hardly up to the task. Chen Quan's methods might have been unconventional, but they endeared him to the brothel set, who considered it all a grand joke.

Notes

1. See note in the introduction on the historical Chen Quan.
2. Reading *pei* 赔 as *pei* 陪.

Type 14
Fake Silver

Planting a Fake Ingot to Swindle a Farmer

There once was a man from a farming family who worked hard at tilling his fields. His dress was plain and his diet meager, for he was miserly by nature, but his family was rather well off. A swindler from another province came to town and learned of this man's greed and foolhardiness. Having determining that the farmer would be tilling his field at a particular spot on a particular day, the swindler buried there two fake silver ingots, each weighing a hundred ounces. The crook waited until the farmer was hard at work tilling to show up on the hillside, looking like he was searching high and low for something. "Hey you!" the farmer called out. "What are you looking for over there?"

"What's it to you what I'm looking for?" came the reply.

So the farmer kept quiet. The crook went on checking out one tree, then another, as if he'd lost something.

The farmer spoke up again. "You look ridiculous, fella. The hill is covered in trees—are you going to check every one?"

"Okay, I won't lie to you," said the crook. "Some years ago my dad was captured by bandits and ended up falling in with them. Eventually he accumulated a lot of silver, but since he couldn't carry it all by himself he buried it in a bunch of different places, which he wrote down on a list. He had planned to retrieve it all, but he died before he had the chance. Now according to the list, there's some under a tree around here, but I don't know which one. It's a good job I ran into you—you can help me look. I'll be happy to share whatever I find with you."

The farmer came over with his hoe to help search, and—lo and behold!—under one of the trees they found the two ingots.

The crook feigned elation. "Since we found silver here, there must be some in the other places as well. I'd be happy to break a piece off for you, but I don't have a hammer and awl handy.

"Since I don't have any place to stash this silver," he continued, "why don't we take it to your place for the time being? Once we've found the rest of it, I'll give you a few ingots as a reward. How does that sound?"

"Great. But we've never met, and if you show up and start coming and going, won't that raise suspicions?"

"Then you should claim that I'm some kind of old friend or relative."

"I know—one of my wife's brothers was sold to a river trader when he was six or seven and we haven't heard from him since. Why not say that you're him and that you've come back to see your sister and brother-in-law?" The farmer told the crook the names of his wife's parents, described their appearance, and shared other relevant details.

When they reached his house, the farmer called his wife out to see her brother. When she saw him, she asked, "Brother, why don't you look anything like me?"

"I've grown different because I've been living in another province with a very different environment," the crook replied.

"What's our father's name? What did he look like? How about our mother? What was her name and what did she look like?" The crook's answers were all accurate.

"What's our uncle's name, and what did he look like?"

"I was young when I left," the crook replied, "and I only remember Mother and Father. I don't remember Uncle."

This convinced her, and she killed a chicken and steamed a fish to make a feast for her brother. The farmer's brothers each treated him to a lavish meal as well.

The crook told his supposed brother-in-law, "I need a little spending money. Could you give me fifteen or sixteen ounces of silver?" So the farmer got together ten-odd ounces of silver and gave them to the crook.

A few days later, the crook showed his "brother-in-law" that according to the list there were more than ten ingots at such-and-such hermitage on such-and-such mountain. The hermitage was deserted, so they packed two baskets of provisions and headed out. The crook had instructed two bandits to lie in wait at the hermitage, and they seized the farmer and bound him to a pillar. The bandits drew cutlasses and repeatedly threatened to kill him, but the crook made a show of dissuading them. "My brother-in-law has been so kind to me. He and his brothers have feasted me with chicken and fish. Please don't kill him!"

The three bandits then consumed all the food and drink and went off.

The farmer shouted at the top of his lungs but to no avail. The following afternoon a herdboy happened to pass by and the farmer screamed for help, so he was finally freed from his bonds and able to return home.

His wife asked, "Why are you only back today? And why isn't my brother with you?"

He answered ruefully, "Shut up about him! Shut up about him!"

So even today someone who's been swindled will use the expression, "Shut up about him!"

Recently, in the Jiangyuan area, a man was involved in a similar swindle, but his wife was smarter. She opened the ingot up with an awl and showed him that it was just a lump of plated tin. So they tied the crook up and beat him and didn't let him go until he'd confessed. If not for his wife's astuteness, that man would have fallen into the same hole as this farmer—better to catch on late than never!

This farmer was well off thanks to his arduous labor and abstemious lifestyle. How could he allow greed to lead him into a bandit's trap that cost him both his money and his pride? His wisdom did not equal that of the woman from Jiangyuan. These are, however, dark times of pervasive deception and rampant criminality. Lately these "bag drop bandits" have swindled a lot of people. There's another technique used in Jiang-Huai,[1] the "sweet talk," that's especially tough to defend against. The bandit asks you a question, and you need only reply to come under his spell—it's some kind of sorcery, and many are its victims. How can the world have fallen so low? Ye who would venture out on the road, let this tale be a warning!

Note

1. The large region in central China between the Yangzi and Huai rivers.

Type 15

Government Underlings

Swindled on the Way Out of a Court Hearing

In a village there lived a widow whose family was the richest in the whole town. She had only one son, named Gan Shu. At age twenty, he had just reached his majority and taken over management of his family's properties, which he oversaw conscientiously.

A certain Lu the Fifth, a man of the same town, twice asked Gan Shu for a loan of silver or grain, but Gan Shu always refused him. Resentful, Lu returned home and hatched a plot with his wife, Ms. Hu, asking her to pose as victim and help frame Gan Shu for rape. She assented. He then got his close friend Zhi the Ninth to serve as a witness and went straight to the branch office of the Surveillance Circuit to lodge a complaint.

The circuit intendant[1] investigated the case personally. First, he asked Ms. Hu, "Why did Gan Shu go to your house?"

"His family's loaded," she replied, "and he has nothing to do all day; he just forces himself on people's wives. He knew my man wouldn't be home, so out of the blue he came over and started flirting. When I wouldn't go along, he hugged me and kissed me and didn't leave even when I started cussing at him. He only ran off when Zhi the Ninth came looking for my husband about some goods they were going to sell."

The intendant then asked Zhi, "What was your purpose in going to Lu the Fifth's house?"

Zhi answered, "Sir, Lu the Fifth and I both make our living as vendors, so I was looking for him to sell some goods when I heard his wife yelling and cussing at someone inside. Then Gan Shu came running out."

The intendant then turned to Gan Shu. "Why were you quarreling with that woman?"

Gan Shu answered, "I never went to their house, so how could we have quarreled? Just ask Lu the Fifth's next-door neighbors and you'll see."

The neighbors all testified that Gan Shu was the son of a widow who would never dare to do anything improper. They added that they'd never heard anything that sounded like an assault and that it had to be a fabrication.

Lu the Fifth persisted: "They're a hugely wealthy family; couldn't they have bought a couple of witnesses?"

The neighbors replied, "We live next door to Gan, and we couldn't tell anything was amiss, but that Zhi the Ninth lives one street over. Chances are *he's* the bought witness."

"Lu the Fifth is a poor commoner," the intendant pointed out, "so he can't afford to buy a witness." Determined to get to the bottom of this alleged rape, he had all of the neighbors and Gan Shu given twenty strokes of the rod apiece.

Gan Shu left the courtroom in a state of terror and apprehension. After the afternoon session had concluded and the courthouse gates had been shut, he walked in aimless circles in the rear courtyard, lost in thought. "Wrong! It's just wrong!" he unconsciously cried out. He circled around a few more times, then pulled up his sleeves and made his way back home.

It so happened that a guard, Tu Shan, had been watching him. Watching his body language and hearing him exclaim, "Wrong!"

Tu divined that it must have to do with the rape case. In the middle of the night Tu climbed the wall of the judicial compound and snuck out. He knocked on the door of Gan Shu's agent, who let him in.[2] Inside he found the disconsolate Gan Shu at his wits' end.

"That matter of yours from today, do you want it sorted out?" Tu asked Gan.

"Yes, I'd do anything!"

"Well, it just so happens that the intendant's brother-in-law is in town, but he'll be leaving again in three days. The most effective way would be to bribe him; do that, have your case heard again tomorrow, and you can be sure of a win."

"That sounds great," Gan said. "How much will it cost?"

"Since it's only a matter of overturning your own case, and no one else is involved, a hundred ounces of silver ought to do it."

"I'll pay a hundred to make sure the case is heard tomorrow."

"The intendant and his brother-in-law are at a banquet that's still going on; I'll head straight over there to have a word with him."

Gan Shu and his agent saw Tu Shan off. The main gate of the court was closed, so Tu climbed in over the wall from the house of a neighboring resident.

The next day, the intendant began the morning session by issuing warrants for further proceedings in the rape case. Gan Shu was delighted, thinking that he had brought this about.

That afternoon, Gan was interrogated again: "Did Lu the Fifth ask you for a loan or not?"

"He asked me twice for loans of silver or grain, and I said no both times. He bore such a grudge that he framed and slandered me."

The intendant questioned Lu's wife further: "How could Gan Shu have raped you if he never went to your house?"

Lu the Fifth's side had not bribed the court attendants, so the finger-squeezers were tightened hard from the very first squeeze. Lu's wife couldn't take it and blurted out the truth, that there had been no rape and that they had filed a false report because Gan Shu had refused to make a loan. Lu the Fifth and Zhi the Ninth were thereupon given thirty blows, and Gan Shu was completely exonerated.

Tu Shan followed him out to collect the promised fee. "I'm more than happy to give it to you," Gan Shu told him. Tu accepted the hundred ounces of silver with such an animated show of appreciation that Gan Shu gave him a further ten ounces.

In addition to the money for getting the intendant to set Gan Shu free, Tu Shan received ten ounces for his enthusiastic gratitude. Gan thought that he had been exonerated thanks to the intercession of the brother-in-law—little did he imagine that the happy outcome was because of the intendant's own change of mind and that he'd been thoroughly swindled by Tu Shan!

Yamen underlings depend on swindling for their very livelihood; it's how they're able to live so comfortably. The volume of their swindles is beyond reckoning. Everything—they swindle! Every day—they swindle! Everyone—they swindle! "More numerous than the bamboo on the southern mountain" are their swindles—you could never count them all! And if Judge Bao himself came back to life, he'd never solve them all![3] *I myself have never set foot in a courtroom, and it's rare for deception of this sort to come to light. I just happened to learn the truth, so I've set down a record of these misdeeds. It's true: everyone in the yamen is a miscreant, and the place is a thicket of swindles. This is why it's imperative to complete your legal obligations in a timely fashion and do your utmost to avoid lawsuits. If you do, even a corrupt clerk or an antagonistic patrolman can't touch you. So I say:*

> *Their plots are far too clever, you'd best not get involved;*
> *that feather wine is toxic, you'd best not touch a drop;*[4]
> *those underlings are tricky, you'd best not get too close.*

Now disasters do happen, in spite of everything, and one can end up in court, in which case one might hope for a brilliant official to clear one's name. Yet to what avail? While officials are all men of learning and thus tend to be enlightened, even they can do nothing about their underlings, who envelop them in clouds of confusion. Whatever small annoyances you may suffer as a result, it's best to stay out of the yamen.

Notes

1. The title *daoti* 道提 used here is not the normal term for the official in charge of a surveillance circuit branch, which oversaw judicial affairs in one portion of a province, usually consisting of several prefectures. The official in question may have been either the *daotai* 道臺, the local circuit intendant, or his superior at the circuit level.
2. Agents (*xiejia* 歇家) were go-betweens in commercial transactions and sometimes in official matters; here the *xiejia* may have been a kind of consigliere or legal advisor.
3. The saying in the first part of the sentence alludes to misdeeds so numerous that they cannot be fully recorded. Judge Bao was a famous eleventh-century official and appears in the next story, "An Officer Reprimands a Captured Criminal in Order to Halve His Flogging."
4. The drink was made with the plumage of the *zhen* 鴆, a legendary bird whose feather turned wine poisonous.

An Officer Reprimands a Captured Criminal in Order to Halve His Flogging

Judge Bao, known posthumously as Bao the Filial and Solemn, enjoys a reputation as an official of incorruptible morals and keen discernment who applied the law impartially. He never allowed deceivers to save themselves with clever rhetoric or criminals to exculpate themselves by recourse to power and status. Nor did he accept inducements. This is why people praised him as follows:

> Bribe and things will not go well
> with Bao, the very King of Hell.

A playboy from a rich family was once caught fornicating and knew that he was unlikely to go unpunished. He therefore hatched a scheme with one of Judge Bao's veteran officers in advance of the court hearing: "His Excellency is a brilliant judge with superhuman powers of investigation. Since in my case there are both witnesses and material evidence, I'm sure to be convicted. If the sentence is severe, while I can pay whatever fine might be imposed, the one thing I really can't endure is flogging. Do you have any strategy that might reduce how much I'm beaten? Money is no object."

The officer replied: "Tomorrow, when your sentence is about to be carried out, run up to the judge's bench and beg for clemency. I'll be right there and I'll curse you out, which will result in me taking some of the beating for you. It might even halve the number of strokes you suffer. That's the best we can do."

The next day, Judge Bao discovered the facts of the case and, in a fury, ordered forty strokes of the rod for the rich scion. The young man immediately ran up to the judge's bench and started babbling about how he should be spared. The senior officer hollered at him from the side: "Go on and take your beating! You've got nothing left to say—you're guilty and you're not getting off!"

Judge Bao was enraged at the sight of a clerk overstepping his authority. *If he were to use this arrogated power to deceive others in the future*, Bao worried, *it would only lead to greater troubles.* He immediately ordered twenty strokes for the officer and deducted twenty strokes from the rich scion's punishment, in order to demonstrate that his officers possessed no authority of their own. Little did he realize that he had fallen for his senior officer's scheme. The officer later received a handsome bribe, and Judge Bao was none the wiser.

Whenever a yamen officer engages in treachery, it's because he understands his chief's character and can manipulate it to his own ends. This experienced officer knew that Judge Bao kept strict discipline and would not brook a petty clerk usurping his authority. So when the clerk rebuked the criminal, Judge Bao would be sure to have him beaten and lighten the criminal's punishment accordingly, in order to demonstrate that his subordinates had no authority and outsiders had no reason to fear them. Unbeknownst to Judge Bao, his underling had schemed to have the flogging split with the criminal to earn a bribe—how could anyone have solved that one? If Judge Bao himself could be duped by his officers, how much more so officials today!

Type 16

Marriage

Marrying a Street Cleaner and Provoking His Death

In the capital lived a man named Fang the Eighth, a dull-witted fellow who made his living cleaning the streets.[1] His household consisted of just himself and his elderly mother.

Once, at the end of a day of cleaning the streets, Fang went over to a stream to wash up. As evening approached, a woman in hempen clothing[2] came along and stood watching him finish. "I'm on my way to my mother's," she told him, "but it's late and I won't make it tonight. Could I spend the night at your house?"

"That won't work. Why don't you try an inn?"

"There are all sorts of people at an inn, so it's not an ideal place. Who else lives at your house?"

"My aged mother."

"You have a mother? Then I can sleep next to her."

Fang led her home, and the woman gave him money to buy rice, wine, and some take-out dishes. That night the three of them dined together.

The woman asked whether he had ever been married. Fang's mother answered, "We barely manage to get by. We could never find the money for a wedding."

The woman said, "My husband passed away and I just buried him. He had no relatives, so I had to pack up my belongings and head back to my mother's house, which is a long way from here. Your son seems very kind and devoted, so our chance meeting must be by divine providence. I'd like to become your daughter-in-law and serve you day and night. What do you think?"

"I appreciate the sentiment, but I fear my son wouldn't be able to provide for three people."

"I'd bring a little silver with me, and I can support myself doing women's work."[3]

Fang was delighted. "I had my fortune told this year and I was supposed to find a good wife. If we're both bringing in income, it won't matter that I can't support you by myself."

That night they slept together as bride and groom—a night of untrammeled passion. For the longtime bachelor it was like nectar after thirst; for the "lonesome widow" it was like coolness after sweltering heat. They made love like fish cavorting in water. Fang's mother too was delighted that Heaven had bestowed upon her such a virtuous daughter-in-law.

The next day, the woman gave her husband six tenths of an ounce of silver to buy rice, prepared food, and vegetables. The day after that, she asked her mother-in-law, "Why don't we make a set of clothes?" The mother said she had no money, so the woman got out another six tenths of an ounce and told her husband to go make a purchase at Merchant Wang's Cloth Emporium. Fang did so, and his wife made some clothes and earned some money. He was overjoyed. He went to Wang's store again and bought two lengths of green cloth. He brought them home to his wife and she cut three inches off each. Then she held up a ruler and said, "This cloth is short; it's not a full length. Who would be fooled by this? You should take it back and exchange it. We paid good money for it; how can they behave so shamefully!"

Fang obeyed and went to return it. At Wang's Emporium, they said, "This store never sells anyone short. You must have cut it to fool with us." The two argued back and forth for a while, before finally Merchant Wang had a family member give Fang two measures of cloth.

Fang brought it back to his wife, who secretly poked several holes in it with a knife. She unrolled it and said, "How could they give you back this mangled stuff? That store is despicable; they're only cheating you because they think they can take advantage of your good nature. If they won't exchange it this time, you should really have it out with them. What do you have to fear from them?"

Riled up by his wife, Fang went back in a huff and said, "You cheated me with damaged cloth!"

"Why would we go to the trouble of letting you exchange the same cloth again and again!" Merchant Wang exclaimed, and refused to exchange it. Fang cursed and cussed; Wang got angry too, and told his family to give Fang a beating. Then they took two bolts of cloth, unrolled them so he could see them clearly, and tossed them at him.

Fang went back home with the cloth and said how upset he was at the beating. His wife stamped her feet in anger. "You had money and bought cloth, but you ended up with a beating. He's relying on his wealth and status. We have to fight him to the bitter end. Your mom and I can plead for justice on your behalf."

Again, Fang was riled up by her talk and went back to the store in a froth. And again, Wang's family members banded together and gave him a thrashing. He returned home badly injured. His wife, in tears, said, "You must report this crime!" So he went to the office of the censor to file a complaint. When he returned she bought some fine wine and fine food, and urged her husband to drink liberally to loosen his blood flow. He complied and drank himself into a stupor. That night, taking advantage of his inebriation, she bound his hands and feet and plugged up his nose and mouth with sand.

By the third watch he was long dead. After undoing his bonds, she screamed, "Your son's body's cold and stiff—is he dead?!" The mother, startled awake, saw that her son was indeed deceased. The two of them wailed in grief. Then they went back to the censor's office to amend the complaint. An official was dispatched to verify the situation and collect evidence; he found the body covered in grievous wounds. Merchant Wang, stunned and in a panic, was dumbfounded.

Three days later, with a verdict looming, the widow went to Wang's store with her mother-in-law and said, "Since you've beaten my husband to death, my elderly mother-in-law and I will have a hard time providing for ourselves. It would be pointless to have you pay with your life; if you could offer three hundred ounces of silver to support my mother-in-law, I could tell her to drop the charges and have the investigation ended."

Merchant Wang was pleased to hear this and had his people draw up an agreement that provided two hundred ounces for the support of Fang's mother. Fang's mother agreed and dropped the case, saying that she was old, her son dead, and her daughter-in-law a widow, and that she had no means of support. At the urging of his relatives and neighbors, Wang gave another hundred ounces to the Fang family to support her.

The authorities agreed to drop the case, though they gave Merchant Wang twenty strokes of the cane as punishment for his crime. They sent Fang's wife home with the silver, but after two days she had run off in the night with two hundred ounces of it. No one knew where she had gone. Fang's mother wanted to report it, but Merchant Wang gave her another twenty ounces to put an end to the affair.

This woman was the wife of a major crook. He studied Fang, discovered that he had only an elderly mother, then sent his wife to marry him under false pretenses. After provoking him into getting beaten up at the shop of a wealthy man, she engineered his death. Fang's mother, of course, would have to report it, and they would be sure of receiving some silver. Then the wife would abscond with the lot. This is a case of a crook so treacherous that he would send a man to his death for the sake of profit, and of a man so simple-minded that he fell into the trap.

Notes

1. Zhang Yingyu signals one moral of this story through some complex wordplay. *Taojie* 淘街 (literally "street washing") is not the standard term for street cleaning. *Taojie*, in combination with the name Fang the Eighth (Fang Ba 方八), calls to mind the expression *pajie taokong* 扒街淘空 (literally, "to crawl along the street until you've washed it clean"), meaning to find fault persistently and unfairly, and thereby bring misfortune upon oneself. (The first character in the phrase incorporates the graph 八 ["eight"] that appears in the protagonist's given name and can also be pronounced *ba*.) Zhang Yingyu reused this bit of wordplay later in *The Book of Swindles*: another street cleaner (*taojie*), named Ban the Eighth (Ban Ba 班八), is a character in the final story in the "Sorcery" section, "Molian zei guaidai youtong" 摩臉賊拐帶幼童 ("A Villain Kidnaps Boys by Touching Their Face"), not translated in this volume. The near-synonym *taolu* 淘路 ("road cleaning") also sounds like *taolu* 淘碌/漉, a common expression meaning to exhaust one's energy, especially sexually; both this story and the face-touching story feature sex followed by death.

2. Hemp was typically worn by people in mourning.

3. Spinning, weaving, sewing, embroidery, and other textile crafts were considered "women's work."

Taking a Concubine from Another Province Leads to a Disastrous Lawsuit

Cai Tianshou, from Guangdong province, was a man of generous spirit and upright character. At the age of forty he was still childless, but his shrewish wife forbade him from taking a concubine. One day he went to Suzhou to sell thirty-odd loads of Guangdong tin. There, he told his broker Xiao Hanqing, "I have no children yet, so I'd like to take a concubine here. Do you think there'd be anyone suitable?"

"So long as you've got the money, you're sure to find a girl to your liking," Xiao replied.

Xiao took Cai to see several young maidens, but Cai said, "I'm over forty. These girls are all too young for me, so they won't do."

There happened to be an idler named Guo Yanji whose mother, Ms. Deng, was a thirty-three-year-old widow of pleasing appearance. Her husband's death had left her with an inheritance of a thousand ounces of silver, but Guo had gambled this down to nothing and accrued twenty-plus ounces in gambling debts besides.

Hard-pressed by creditors, he made a deal with a crook: he would pretend that his mother was his wife, whom he wished to marry off to pay his debts. A matchmaker contacted Xiao Hanqing, who brought Cai to see her. Her age and appearance were both to Cai's liking, so he negotiated a bride-price of forty ounces of silver.

Guo Yanji advised him: "This woman comes from a place north of the river, and I fear that her natal family will prevent her from marrying into a household at such great remove. Why don't you seal up the silver and give it to the broker; then when you're about to depart I'll have her board the boat, and you can hand over the silver right then."

The broker agreed to this. When Cai was ready to leave, Guo hired a sedan chair, claiming to be taking Ms. Deng to visit her brother's family. Not until she had boarded the boat did she realize that her son was marrying her off to a traveling merchant. Though incensed, she kept her cool and asked, "Well, since my husband is marrying me off, there's no need to deceive me. Who's my new husband?"

"This unworthy man," said Cai.

"You look rich, at least," replied his bride, "so I don't mind. But the thing is, since my old husband would just gamble everything away, I kept all my clothes and jewelry at my parents' house. Can we go pick them up, and also tell my family about us?"

Cai believed her, so he accompanied her there. When she arrived, she angrily explained to her family that her son had betrayed her by marrying her off.

Her elder brother Deng Tianming was furious. "What kind of son marries his mother off?! And just what sort of traveling merchant is this who has the gall to marry you?" He went out and started raining blows on Cai Tianshou.

Ms. Deng came to Cai's defense, saying, "Forgive him—he was just as much in the dark as I was. It's that unfilial Yanji who deserves to die for his impudence!"

Deng Tianming went straight to the county yamen to file a complaint, and Venerable Zou took the case. He sent men to bring in Guo, but Guo had fled, so he had Xiao Hanqing and Cai Tianshou appear before him first. He interrogated them angrily, ordering twenty blows each for the groom and the matchmaker. Then he threw Cai in jail and made Xiao responsible for catching Guo Yanji. Several months went by and Xiao, still unable to find Guo, was repeatedly flogged for missing deadlines for the latter's capture. Cai tried to bribe his way out of prison, but Venerable Zou could not be bought. Then someone advised Cai, "It takes a thief to catch a thief and a gambler to catch a gambler. Why not pay a crooked gambler to catch him?"

Within a few days, the crook revealed Guo's whereabouts, and Venerable Zou dispatched men to seize him. For marrying his mother off to become the concubine of some far-flung traveler, Venerable Zou sentenced Guo Yanji to a heavy punishment of forty blows. The bride-price was confiscated by the state, and Xiao and Cai were given further beatings. Guo's mother, Ms. Deng, was put under the care of her brother, Deng Tianming, and issued a certificate allowing her to remarry at her own discretion.

Taking a concubine to obtain an heir is not forbidden by the standards of propriety, but one ought to marry from a lesser household in one's vicinity. Marrying outside one's province in such murky circumstances is asking for trouble. This case offers an unmistakable warning.

Type 17
Illicit Passion

A Geomancer Uses His Wife to
Steal a Good Seed

Geomancer Lu was skilled in finding auspicious grave sites. His search for a good plot to bury his father took him all the way to the walled town of Ning,[1] where he found a place with excellent fengshui located behind the tomb altar of Magistrate Yang. The plot was as difficult to buy in the open market as it would have been to steal for an unauthorized burial. When he heard that the magistrate had passed on, and that his two sons were looking for a place to bury their father, Geomancer Lu duly suggested to them the parcel he had planned to use for his own father. He took them to see it and they found it much to their liking. It was a propitious location surrounded by hills and facing in the right direction, and moreover they wouldn't have to go to the trouble of purchasing it. They thus buried Magistrate Yang there and compensated Lu with thirty ounces of silver.

Lu, unable to acquire their land, decided to steal their seed instead. He therefore rented a house close to the Masters Yang's garden and used the silver he'd earned to buy himself a beautiful wife.

Lu and his new wife had been living together for two months when he told her: "I'm going off to ply my fengshui trade and I can't know for sure when I'll be back. If you find yourself running low on fuel or rice, know that I've already asked the Masters Yang to look out for you. These men are great benefactors of mine—it was money I received from them that enabled me to marry you. Should one or both of them make advances toward you while I'm away, it's all right for you to let him have his way. If one of the Yang brothers becomes emotionally attached to you, he's certain to provide for you generously. But whatever you do, avoid relations with any of their many household slaves or servants. Give yourself away lightly and the masters will look down on you. If you were to fall into poverty or get into some other kind of trouble, you couldn't expect them to bail you out."

Lu then made a request of the Yang brothers: "I'll be traveling outside the county for a while, and my household is tiny, so I'm leaving my family's welfare in your hands. I'll reimburse any expense you may incur upon my return."

The Yang brothers, who often visited the garden, had already noticed how beautiful Mrs. Lu was and had thought of making advances. Just two days after Lu's departure, the elder brother went to his house and made a pass at his wife. Following her husband's instructions, she accepted him with alacrity, and soon the two had formed a close emotional bond. A little over a month later, the younger brother also came and made a pass at her, and again she accepted the advances.

When Geomancer Lu returned half a year later, he found his house amply stocked with the basic necessities.

"Did the Masters Yang visit you?" he asked his wife.

"Both of them came, and I welcomed them both."

"There's no shame in you associating with such good men," he told her. "You'll have enough to eat and wear and you won't have to sleep alone. Knowing that someone is always watching out for you while I'm away, my mind will be at ease no matter how far my travels take me."

His wife smiled. "I'm better provided for than when you're home—just don't get jealous."

"I married you using their money, and now they're supporting you on my behalf—why would I be jealous? That said, with two of them repeatedly visiting you I'm worried that you might end up poisoning the relationship between them. You'll need to avoid this by setting a schedule whereby they visit you on alternate months."

The next time Lu went on a trip, the Yang brothers sought out his wife again. This time she told them: "If you two keep visiting me on an irregular basis I'm worried that I'll end up becoming an open wound on your brotherly relationship. Let's set a schedule that has elder brother visiting me in odd months and younger brother in even months."

"You're right," they said. "From now on, one of us will provide for you one month and the other will do so the next."

In a flash, four years had gone by and Mrs. Lu had given birth to two sons, both of the Yang bloodline. Geomancer Lu had the sons' fortunes told: both were destined for great wealth and high rank. He thereupon moved back to his hometown with his wife and sons, taking leave of the Yang brothers, each of whom gave him generous gifts for his journey.

Later, both his sons went on to pass the civil service examinations. In truth, he had drained away the Yang clan's fengshui and left them none the wiser.

The scions of wealthy and noble families often defile other people's wives and daughters, some even fathering offspring by them. This inevitably results in their fengshui being divided and depleted. Let this geomancer's seed stealing serve as a warning to future generations.

Once there was a scion of a wealthy family who, encountering the beautiful wife of a tenant farmer while making the rounds to collect the rent, repeatedly tried to seduce her. She didn't dare accede to his advances, but when she confided to her mother-in-law about what was going on, her mother-in-law told her: "He's from a rich family. If you were to have a son by him, you'd eat well for the rest of your life."

The next time the rich son tried to seduce her she gave in. "You've rejected me so many times," he said, as they were undressing in the bedroom. "What made you change your mind?"

"I talked it over with my mother-in-law."

"Is she planning to catch us in the act?"

"Far from it! She said that if I had a son by a rich man's seed, I'd never lack for food."

Hearing her speak about him losing his seed, the man abruptly reconsidered what he was doing and blurted out: "Absolutely not! Absolutely not!"

Those four words no sooner escaped his lips than he completely changed his tune: "I wasn't really looking for an affair. I was just taken by your beauty and wanted to flirt. Here's three tenths of an ounce of silver for you to buy some makeup. I won't dishonor you."

His lust aroused, he raced home and had sex with his wife, who got pregnant that very night. She later gave birth to a boy who passed the metropolitan examinations to become a *jinshi* and was appointed to the post of county magistrate.

The day the son took up his official appointment the weather was clear and fair. On each of the two pillars flanking the main hall of the yamen he saw two characters in gold: *Absolutely not*. This made him uneasy, and he thought: *This means that I absolutely must not serve in this post!* For three months, he carried out his duties conscientiously. He then resigned his post, claiming illness and the need to go home to take care of his aging parents.

When he suddenly appeared at home, his father was startled to see him. "Why are you back?"

"Because on the very day I assumed my post I saw two sets of gilded characters, each reading, 'Absolutely not.' I feared that it was an inauspicious omen and resigned my post to care for you."

"But it's perfectly normal to take care of one's parents while still in office," his father pointed out.

During the night the father had a revelation and called his son to him. "Those golden characters you saw reading 'Absolutely not' are an extremely auspicious omen that you are sure to rise to high office. In my youth I once dallied with the wife of one of our tenant farmers. She was willing, but just before we were going to do it she told me she coveted my superior seed. That brought me to my senses and I blurted out, 'Absolutely not! Absolutely not!' and refused to consummate it. That night I went home and conceived you with your mother. Clearly, Heaven is rewarding me for having the virtue not to defile another man's wife. If it were an ill omen, why would it be written in gold? And why would those four words be precisely the ones I uttered back then? This is a most excellent sign."

"I agree," his son replied. He thereupon wrote to classmates who had passed the examination in the same year and, with their assistance, managed to resume his post the following year. Later he became a vice minister and brought great status and prosperity to his house.

This anecdote makes it clear why the scions of rich and noble families must not lose their seed to other families.

Once there was a county magistrate with four sons, all of whom had earned the degree of *xiucai* and were intelligent men of noble bearing. One day, the magistrate passed away. A geomancer chose a burial plot with excellent fengshui and informed the magistrate's sons: "Within the next six years, in one of the next two rounds, all four of you will pass the metropolitan examinations."

Six years later, the geomancer returned to receive their thanks. The three eldest brothers had passed the exam and were off serving as officials. Only the youngest brother was left at home. He received the geomancer cordially and asked, "You predicted that all four brothers would pass the metropolitan examination, and so far three of us have fulfilled that prediction. In terms of sheer talent I surpass my brothers, yet I alone have failed to pass. Why is this?"

The next day, the geomancer and the fourth brother went to reexamine the father's grave site. "Based on this topography, all four of you should have passed. There must be a reason you didn't."

The fourth son implored him to reveal the truth. "How old was your father when you were born?" the geomancer asked by way of reply.

"He was sixty when I was born, and he passed away at seventy-four. That was six years ago."

"And your mother, how old was she?"

"She was thirty."

The geomancer shook his head. "I knew it."

"Knew what, sir?"

"Now, don't blame me for saying this: if you really are set on passing the examination, you'll have to ask your mother about your true bloodline."

The young master caught his drift. That night he arranged a lavish dinner, during which he gently but persistently pressed wine on his mother until she became drunk. After the second watch, he sent family members and servants off to sleep, and, when they were alone, he knelt down before his mother. "Your son is troubled by something but dares not speak of it. Tell me, Mother: do you want me to pass the examination or not?"

His mother replied, "Your three elder brothers all passed, and I want nothing more than for you to pass too. What is it? You can tell me anything, be it good or ill."

"The geomancer said that I didn't pass because I'm not of Dad's bloodline. I have to know who my real father is if I'm to pass the exam."

The mother had always adored her youngest son, it was the dead of night, no one else was around, and she was drunk, so she blurted out: "The geomancer is as wise as they say! Your father was already sixty when I met a good-looking young man who was working in the county government office. He was the son of a high minister. I had you with him."

Having learned the truth, the fourth son discussed it the next day with the geomancer, who advised him: "You'll have to go to where the remains of the minister's son are buried and find a way to exhume them and rebury them next to your father's coffin. Do that and you'll pass in the next round."

The fourth son did as instructed, exhuming and reburying his real father's remains, and the next time the metropolitan examinations were held, sure enough, he passed.

This anecdote reveals the consequences of conceiving a bastard in secret and leaving the illegitimate son in the dark. When people separated by rank share the same fengshui, awkward secrets are inevitable.

Then there is the case of a certain Xie, whose father was of weak constitution and without offspring. During a blazing hot summer night, his wife lay asleep in bed covered only by a light skirt when a monkey that the family kept as a pet came in and started raping her. Startled awake, she tried to push it off, but the monkey tried to bite and scratch her and she was unable to push it away. She fell into a deep sleep in which her spirit became aroused and her lust was unconsciously excited; as a result, she became pregnant. When her husband returned home she told him of having been raped by the monkey.

"That monster!" he exclaimed. "It must be killed."

The monkey, feeling guilty about the rape, had climbed up a big peach tree by the back door and refused to come down. To lure it down, Xie's father dallied with his wife under the tree. The monkey, seeing how happy they looked, finally climbed down. Xie's father then clubbed it to death and buried it at the base of the tree.

Xie, once he was born, turned out to be a clever lad nimble of both mind and body. Seeing him jump and tumble about like a monkey, Xie's mother knew in her heart that he was the product of the monkey's seed. As she had no other children, however, she decided not to kill him. When Xie was eight years old his father died. The geomancer who chose the burial site told the widow: "This site is excellent—it guarantees that your son will grow to become a child prodigy. Though he's not bright right now, in three years he'll pass the examinations with flying colors."

Three years later, the geomancer returned.

"You told me that in three years my son would change, but he's still as unserious and wild as ever. What am I to do?"

The geomancer visited the father's grave again and gave it a careful look over. He then went back and asked the woman, "Did you bear this boy yourself, or was he born of a concubine?"

"He's not my real flesh and blood," she replied. "A serving girl from a neighbor's house conceived him with a monkey and wanted to abandon him. Since I had no children myself, I decided to raise him as my own."

"If you want this boy to realize his potential," the geomancer advised her, "you'll need to get hold of the monkey's remains and bury them beside this tomb. It will bring prosperity to your family."

Xie's mother found the monkey's skeleton still buried beneath the peach tree. She dug it up and brought it to the geomancer, "The neighbor still had the remains. Where should they go?"

The geomancer chose an auspicious day and reinterred them. Three years later, sure enough, Xie passed the examinations and was hailed as a child prodigy. He went on to achieve great renown.

(This story was related to me by Geomancer Chen, of Xie's home county.)

This anecdote shows how quickly and powerfully fengshui takes effect. Even if you secure the right plot of land, your descendants must observe proper moral conduct and avoid lust and depravity at all costs, lest your bloodline drain into another.

Note

1. Ningcheng 寧城 most likely refers either to the seat of Jianning county or to the seat of Jianning prefecture, both in northern Fujian province.

Type 18

Women

Coaxing a Sister-in-Law Into Adultery to Scam Oil and Meat

A woman and her sister-in-law were sitting together when an oil seller happened by. The woman, née Shi, remarked, "We're out of cooking oil at home. Too bad we don't have any money to buy some."

Her sister-in-law, née Zuo, the wife of her husband's elder brother, replied, "Buy a measure of oil on credit and arrange to pay later."

Ms. Shi called the oil seller into the house and asked for two pounds of oil. She then said to the peddler, "My man isn't at home at the moment. Come back for the money in two days."

Two days later the oil seller returned.

"I have no money. What should I do?" Shi asked Zuo.

"Tell him to come back in another three days," Zuo replied.

Shi put him off as suggested. Three days later she complained to her sister-in-law, "You told me to go ahead and buy the oil, but we still have no money. Go and borrow some so that I can repay this debt."

"If you're willing to do as I instruct, you'll have no problem repaying him," Zuo replied.

"I've always taken my cues from you. What should I do?"

"That oil seller seems like a handsome young man, and you're a beautiful young woman. I'd bet that if you were to sleep with him once he wouldn't ask for the oil money."

"You wouldn't blab?"

"I'm the one telling you to do this, so I wouldn't dare say anything. I'll just hide in the house while you take care of business."

Before long the oil seller arrived. Ms. Shi, figuring that there was no other way out, forced a smile and went out to greet him.

"I've asked you to come for the money twice now, but I haven't been able to pay you either time. Maybe it'd be best if you took me for payment."

The oil seller's lust was aroused by her inviting smile, but he balked.

"Don't try to fool me—you're not home alone."

"My husband is off plowing the fields and my elder sister-in-law is off spinning hemp at a neighbor's. I'm only being this forward because no one's home."

This put the oil seller's mind at ease, and he followed her into the bedroom.

Hearing the bedroom door shut, Ms. Zuo snuck out of her hiding place and poured half of the oil from each of the peddler's shoulder-pole buckets into her own container and replaced it with the same volume of water. Then she went back to the bedroom door to eavesdrop.

"You've finished," she overheard her sister-in-law saying. "You should be off."

"Let me stay with you a little longer," the oil seller said.

Ms. Zuo picked up her basket of hemp and hurried out the front door, where she called out in an intentionally loud voice: "It's not even noon! Back from the fields so early?"

The oil seller, overhearing this, raced out to shoulder his buckets and bumped into Ms. Zuo at the front door.

"Did the missus pay you for the oil?" she asked.

"Yes! Yes!" he hurriedly replied, and raced off to the next village.

Ms. Zuo knew that he'd be back and stood waiting for him by the front door. Sure enough, around midday she saw the oil seller approaching. "You still here?" she asked. "My sister-in-law's younger brother came here with some buckets to draw water and found a carrying pole and two buckets of oil in the house. He didn't see anyone around but heard the sound of laughter and chitchat coming from inside his sister's bedroom. He suspected that the oil seller was carrying on with his sister, so he poured the oil into his own buckets and refilled yours with water. He then went to get his mother, and they raced over together to catch the adulterers in the act. By the time they got here you'd gone, and they were just here discussing their suspicions. If they knew you were around they'd settle scores with you for sure."

The oil seller was about to make himself scarce when Ms. Zuo stopped him.

"You ought to thank me for tipping you off."

"I'll send you two pounds of oil tomorrow," he replied.

After the promised oil arrived a few days later, Ms. Zuo changed her story again. Taking the oil to Ms. Shi, she said, "The other day I was standing at the front door when the oil seller passed by, and I teased him by saying: 'My sister-in-law told me that she isn't done paying you for the oil and that there must be some reason you said she'd paid in full when you left in such a rush. I thought you might like to know.' He felt so guilty that he promised me two pounds of oil, which were delivered today. You're the one who earned it, so I owe it to you."

"It looks like those few moments of my time were worth four pounds of cooking oil. Thanks for teaching me that," Shi said.

"If you do as I say," Zuo replied, "there'll be more good things to come."

A short while later they heard the sound of a man hawking fresh meat. They called him in and had him measure out two pounds apiece, telling him to come back another day for the money. Three days later, the butcher came by to collect. Ms. Zuo weighed out seven hundredths of an ounce of silver and told him to come back in two days to collect the money her sister-in-law owed.

On the appointed day the butcher came back, and Zuo said to Shi: "You pay him back with the same trick as last time; I'll position myself at a convenient spot inside."

Ms. Shi came out and greeted the butcher with a smile. "I borrowed meat from you without having any money to pay you back. No one else is home today. How about I pay for flesh with flesh?"

The butcher leered at the beauty before him.

"I'd be happy with just a certain piece of flesh around your middle."

"I'm offering you the lot," Ms. Shi replied. "Why settle for so little?"

The butcher carried her into the bedroom to do the deed. Zuo snuck out and removed all of the peddler's meat. Then she sat down quietly next to the empty shoulder-pole buckets.

After the butcher had taken his pleasure with Ms. Shi, he came back out.

"Where did all my meat go?"

"Her husband took it to the village elders," Zuo replied.

"How could he have stolen my meat?"

"You have some nerve! Her husband came home and saw a carrying pole loaded with meat here, then went in and found the bedroom door shut tight. Hearing two people giggling and carrying on inside, he knew that you were fornicating with his wife and told me to guard the bedroom door. I couldn't very well listen in on your antics, which is why I'm sitting here. Have a seat for a moment, and the man who stole your meat will be right back."

The butcher shouldered his empty buckets and was about to flee when Ms. Zuo grabbed him, saying, "Give me your cleaver and I'll let you go."

"If it's all right with you, I'll give you two pounds of meat tomorrow instead."

Zuo released the butcher, who sped off.

Ms. Shi was upset. "You put me up to this! Now my husband knows what's going on—what good can come of that?"

"I wouldn't drag your husband into this if I were you. So long as you're willing to eat meat, this affair won't be hard to cover up."

"What's the plan? Out with it, quick!"

Zuo went inside and hauled out an entire leg, then pulled out another leg. "Would you prefer to eat meat or tell your husband?"

"You stole his meat! You shouldn't scare me to death like that!"

"The butcher's the one I wanted to scare; if I hadn't, we wouldn't have gotten all this meat."

The two women stewed some of the meat and sat down to eat it with wine. Ms. Shi remarked, "Know what this is called? One day of shamelessness for three days of a full belly."

"I'd hardly say that," Zuo said. "It's more like a moment of delight followed by a month of wine and meat!"

The two burst out laughing and ate their fill. The meat they couldn't finish they smoked as jerky.

Several days later the butcher passed by and Ms. Zuo went out to meet him. She indicated two pounds of meat and the butcher cut it for her promptly.

"Thanks to you my sister-in-law suffered a vicious beating the other day," Zuo told him. "You should give her two pounds too."

The butcher duly cut off another slab and said, "Give this to her for me—I'm too busy to do it myself."

Zuo carried the two slabs of meat inside and passed the message to Shi, adding that there was more fun to be had in the future. Shi remarked, "I make a pretty good adulteress, but you make an even better crook."

With that, the door to adultery was thrown wide open, and the men who walked through it were too many to record.

Ms. Shi was merely a stupid woman, but Ms. Zuo was a crafty one. Had she been a man, she would have become a major crook. Encountering such an ingenious woman, what simple-minded person would not fall for her schemes? This is why it is not only men who should be selective in their social contacts; women too must choose female companions of the highest integrity.

Three Women Ride Off on Three Horses

Many people living along the Jingnan road keep horses to rent to travelers by the day. One day, three women traveling together without luggage came across a stableman returning home with three horses. Each rented one to ride.

"Auntie is the most skilled rider and should ride in front," the youngest said. "The two of us don't ride so well and will follow behind."

Before they had even gone a single *li*, the young woman called to the stableman to help her down off her horse so that she could go pee. The stableman clasped her tightly as he helped her down, making a pass at her.

"Trying to cop a feel, are you?" she asked.

"I wouldn't dare," the stableman replied. "I was just holding on tight so that you wouldn't fall."

"Looked to me like you were getting fresh. I don't mind your squeezing—my husband's long gone."

"In that case, there's a small thatched hut up ahead. How about a cuddle?"

"We're in a hurry. How about if we take a rest at your place tonight?"

"I don't have three beds."

"My aunts will share a bed, and I'll sleep beside them."

"If you sleep beside me I'll waive the horse rental fee."

"A person's worth more than a horse. You're angling for a bargain again."

"We'd both come out ahead on the deal."

As the two were planning their secret rendezvous, Second Aunt fell off her horse.

"Quick," the woman directed the stableman, "go and help my younger aunt back up."

As he walked ahead, the stableman looked back in her direction. "Don't you play games with me, now."

"If my aunt's hurt herself, she'll need a place to rest en route, won't she? Our date is a sure thing."

The stableman raced ahead to where Second Aunt was sitting in the road with her legs crossed, holding her foot.

"I've hurt my foot and my leg," she told him.

The stableman helped her back up onto her horse. "We've got to get going."

"They're sprained," Second Aunt said. "You'll have to go ahead and buy medicated plasters for them. I won't be able to keep up, so I'll have to rest here by the roadside. You go on ahead and tell First Aunt to wait."

Due to the two delays, the first horse was already more than ten *li* ahead. After the stableman had gone off in pursuit, the two other women vaulted onto their horses and whipped them to gallop off in the opposite direction.

After a while, the stableman anxiously reconsidered. *Let her go on ahead, and I'll wait here for the other two.* Naturally, he was looking forward to sharing a "rest." But a long time passed with no sign of them, and his anxiety mounted. *They must have gone back the other way to buy ointment*, he told himself.

He asked a passerby: "Did you see two women on horseback go by?"

"Two of them flew past—they'd be over twenty *li* from here by now."

"Were they coming this direction or going the other way?"

"They were going the other way. Even if you hurried, you'd never catch them."

Dumbfounded, the stableman hastily retraced his steps, questioning passersby along the way. The story from each was the same: the horses were long gone. He chased them for ten more *li*, but by that time it was getting dark, and passersby now told him that they hadn't seen any women on horses. Three of his horses had been stolen in two directions along the road and he couldn't retrieve a single one. Dejected, he returned home.

The brilliance of this theft lies entirely with the woman at the back who went to pee and then had a tête-à-tête with the stableman, both to ensnare his heart and to tie up his time. Having the middle woman fall from the horse was also clever because it led him to believe that she truly was a poor rider. This too tied up his time, allowing the lead rider to get away free and clear. They tricked him into giving chase because he had no hope of ever catching up.

As for the two women who fled in the opposite direction, he assumed that they were taking so long because of the injury. It never occurred to him that they'd speed off like that. But that stableman was done in partly by infatuation. Why on earth would someone he'd just met on the road agree to sleep with him? Was he so handsome that the woman fell in love with him just like that? It is the sweetest words that are laced with poison. That's why from her honeyed words alone one could tell she was a con woman. If even women can be such master swindlers, what difference is there between our world and that of the demons?

A Buddhist Nun Scatters Prayer Beads to Lure a Woman Into Adultery

Bai Jian's wife, née Xiang, was a radiant beauty. Bai was so fond of his wine, however, that he and his wife were rarely intimate. He worked for the provincial commander, Lord Wang, who dispatched him on business to the capital. Ms. Xiang ran a shop out of their home making paper offerings for funerals. She was assisted by her serving girl, Orchid, whom she often sent out to collect payment and deliver goods. During her husband's long absence Ms. Xiang would often leave the shop to call on friends. A certain Ning Chao-xian saw her on one of these outings and was so transfixed by her beauty that he couldn't stop staring at her. Nor did Ms. Xiang discourage him. Ning went home and conferred with his good friend Cao Zhigao about his desire to seduce this woman.

Cao said, "To dupe a woman you need a woman on the inside—it's the only smooth path to success. As the old saying goes, 'It takes a mountain bandit to beat a mountain bandit, and it takes a pirate to catch a pirate.' In Lotus Sutra Nunnery there's a nun called Miaozhen [Marvelous Truth] who makes the rounds of the local families. If you can get her help, this affair should be a cinch."

Ning was delighted with this intelligence and made his way straight to Lotus Sutra Nunnery. There he met Miaozhen, to whom he conveyed two ounces of silver along with a request that she make contact with Bai Jian's wife at the funerary offerings shop. If she succeeded, he said, he would reward her handsomely.

"No problem at all," the nun told him. "Check back in three days."

Ning carefully went over his instructions, then took his leave of her.

The nun snipped the string of the rosary she always carried, holding the two ends pinched together, and walked past Bai's shop. Having made several passes in front of the shop without spotting Ms. Xiang, she went back to the nunnery with her mission unaccomplished. The next day when she returned, however, she spotted Ms. Xiang sitting in the shop and let the beads slip off the broken string. They scattered all over the ground, and many of them rolled into the mud. The nun had to bend down to gather them up. Ms. Xiang, who witnessed the incident, invited her inside and gave her water to rinse off the beads and wash her hands. The nun thanked her profusely and went on her way.

The next day, the nun bought pastries and cakes and had them delivered to Ms. Xiang's house with her thanks. Ms. Xiang was delighted and sent back an invitation for the nun to join her for a drink and a vegetarian meal, which Miaozhen accepted.

"How old were you when you took your vows?" Ms. Xiang asked during the meal.

"I was already middle-aged."

"What led you to become a nun?"

"I was married to a man who gambled and drank. Since he was never there, it was basically the same as not having a husband. That's why I took vows and became a nun."

Ms. Xiang sighed. "With the guy I got, I'd've been better off not marrying."

The nun, seeing that she'd struck a chord, pressed on. "What makes you sigh like that?"

"I've got the same problem you had. The guy I married is so fond of drinking that he couldn't care less about me. We enjoyed each other's company no more than a few times a year to begin with, and now he's off on a business trip—it's like I don't even have a husband!"

Miaozhen could tell that this woman had springtime yearnings and sought to encourage them further. "Most men are rascals. The only exception I know is Ning Chaoxian, who lives across from the nunnery. He loved his wife more than life itself, but unfortunately she died young. He's recently hired me to help him choose a second wife. That happy woman will thank her lucky stars every day."

Ms. Xiang didn't say anything to this, so the nun couldn't very well keep enticing her. She finished her wine and took her leave.

The next day, Ning dressed in his finest outfit and went to the nunnery to ask what the response had been.

"We're nearly there," Miaozhen told him. "When a wife is on good terms with her husband, she's virtually impossible to seduce. Ms. Xiang had me over yesterday, and I learned that she secretly despises her husband and that he's been away for a long time now. As soon as the opportunity arises she'll fall right into your hands. What you need to do now is to give me some money to arrange a fancy dinner for her at the nunnery. I'll get her drunk on fine wine and she'll be sure to fall asleep on my bed. Then you can undress her and take her gently as you like. When she awakes you must ply her with jewelry like bracelets, hair ornaments, hair clips, and earrings. This way you can buy her affection and ensure that this affair lasts."

Ning bowed to the nun. "If that happens, I'll be grateful to you for life! Here's five more ounces of silver to speed your arrangements for the banquet."

Miaozhen sent someone to buy delicacies and fine wine, instructing the chef to prepare an exquisite banquet. She sent a messenger ahead to deliver the dinner invitation before going in person. Ms. Xiang was delighted and came with Orchid by sedan chair. Seeing such a sumptuous banquet laid out, she asked, "Who else have you invited?"

"Only you," Miaozhen replied. "No one else."

"You've gone to such expense!" Ms. Xiang exclaimed. "How could one person eat so much?"

Miaozhen replied, "I have no flesh-and-blood relatives and am so grateful to have a bosom friend like you. I hope that you'll be my sister and confidante."

Ms. Xiang smiled. "I'm happy to be your confidante; too bad we can't scratch each other's itch!"

After drinking a few cups, she remarked, "This wine is so sweet and fragrant—it must have cost a lot!"

"His Excellency Ning sent it the other day, so I don't know what it cost myself." Miaozhen encouraged her to drink more.

Ms. Xiang said, "Wine this sweet goes down too easily. I'm afraid I'm getting tipsy."

The nun replied, "If you're tipsy, you can take a nap in my room and still wake up in time to make it home. I didn't expect you to reach your limit after just a few cups."

"At night when I have insomnia I can often finish a whole bottle—I can't get to sleep without a drink."

"When your husband's at home, just slake your thirst with him and you should be able to sleep."

"I'll confide in you," Ms. Xiang said. "I get drunk, but I still wake up in the middle of the night. But when my husband is home, the moment he touches the bottle he won't touch me. When I wake up it's absolute torture! How am I supposed to deal with this yearning?"

Miaozhen said, "It sounds like your situation with that husband of yours is the same as mine without one. I can struggle through the day, but nights are hard. It's my bitter fate for not having sown the seeds of virtue in my previous lives."

"You said it," Ms. Xiang replied. "I'm going to get good and drunk so that I can forget everything for one night at least."

Before long she was reeling from the wine and sent Orchid home to watch the house while she took a nap on the nun's bed.

Ning saw that Ms. Xiang was asleep and quickly removed her sash. Her body was limp and warm, so he was able to besiege her as he saw fit. He found her delectable. After a short rest he took her again, and still she didn't wake. Ning held her in her stupor until the middle of the night, when she awoke to discover her clothing off and felt the presence of a man. A pleasurable sensation around her waist spread to permeate her whole body.

"Who are you?" she whispered.

"My darling," Ning replied, "you've been on my mind for so long. Today I just had you twice without your knowing. But from tomorrow onward I want us to enjoy ourselves together."

"Your scheme may have succeeded, but don't you let anyone else learn about this."

"Only the nun knows—how could anyone else?"

They slept until the first light of dawn, when Ms. Xiang arose. Ning gave her the bracelets and hair ornaments and then embraced her and kissed her again. Excited, they went another round, and then walked out of the room hand in hand.

Miaozhen was waiting for them and couldn't suppress a laugh. "A fine wine!" she exclaimed.

"A fine scheme!" Xiang rejoined.

"A fine twist of fate!" Ning remarked.

"If everything's so fine," Miaozhen said, "how will you thank me?" Clasping Ning tightly to her, she told him, "I've run my feet sore for you; I want you to thank me yourself!"

"I'm spent at the moment," Ning replied, "but I won't forget to thank you tonight."

"I'll let him thank you every night from now on," Ms. Xiang put in.

"The more often you and I meet, the more I'll thank her," Ning promised.

From then on, Ning and Ms. Xiang saw each other regularly— all thanks to a procuress nun.

Even the chastest of women, without exception, will be led into sin if she encounters and is enticed by a licentious woman. Women are scrupulous about chastity for two reasons only: because they know shame and because they fear exposure. But once a woman loses her chastity, her sense of shame goes with it—and then she's capable of anything. This is why one should avoid all contact with nuns, matchmakers, and their ilk. Beware the slippery slope off the true path.

Type 19
Kidnapping

A Eunuch Cooks Boys to Make a Tonic
of Male Essence

Court officials, persuaded by glib and specious arguments, appoint eunuchs to travel the empire and collect taxes from merchants. Ostensibly these taxes further the policy of using commerce to support agriculture, but that is merely a pretext. Merchants who are subjected to heavier taxes are inevitably forced to sell at higher prices, thus increasing the cost to buyers, who then suffer losses. Commerce is impeded, and goods-producing regions inevitably become impoverished. Prices decline and sellers suffer losses in turn. Thus, although this profit supposedly comes only from merchants, all four classes of people—scholars, peasants, artisans, and merchants—see their wealth decline as it is surreptitiously appropriated by the court. The harm to the people is even more egregious than would result from openly increasing the agricultural tax.

As for profits deriving from this taxation scheme, for every ounce of silver that makes it into the imperial treasury, eunuchs pocket ten, revenue officials a hundred, and yamen runners a thousand. In short, people expend thousands just to bring the court a single ounce of revenue. The emperor on high benefits little while the people below suffer immeasurable harm.

Yamen runners and revenue officials are, of course, insatiable, yet with just them the people still manage to get by. The problem with those passive parasites of the realm is that they neither till nor weave and just feast off the labors of the populace.

Eunuchs, however, are even more excessive in their predations. They amass enormous fortunes: brocades and silks to them are like leaves beneath their feet; gold and jade tile their homes; the very implements they eat with are identical to the emperor's; and they have subordinates waiting on them like the Son of Heaven himself. They luxuriate in every pleasure known to humankind, their only regret being their inability to debauch women. They lack only that one thing! This is why they are wont to dispatch assistants to seek out and spend enormous sums on tonics for regenerating the male organ.

A certain unorthodox Daoist, with an eye to the money he could make from these eunuchs, trumpeted the spurious claim that "According to ancient prescriptions: 'A deficiency on the part of earth calls for an earth remedy; a deficiency on the part of wood calls for a wood remedy; and a deficiency in the part of a human calls for a human remedy.' In other words, a human can be made whole only by consuming human flesh." He went around offering a made-up recipe that read as follows:

Cook a young boy, mince his liver, dry his flesh into jerky, and consume his vital marrow. This will cause the semen to replenish and the male organ to regenerate so well that you will even be able to have relations with women and father children.

Eunuch Gao, from Fujian province, believed in this prescription and paid the Daoist one hundred ounces of silver for a trial dose. He promised that if it worked the Daoist could claim a reward of ten thousand. He thereupon ordered his henchmen—his fangs and claws—to travel to poor counties and remote villages to buy young boys from impoverished commoners. These henchmen would lie to the father, saying that the Honorable Gao wanted to raise the boy as his own son. In time, they promised, the son would enjoy boundless wealth and honor. Many a poor peasant believed the messenger and sold his son in return for the generous compensation offered and in hopes of future wealth and rank. Countless boys were purchased this way. Some families subsequently had people make inquiries about the son they had sold, but there was never any news. Even the runners in Gao's own offices had no knowledge of the boys being raised in the residential compound.

In fact, the eunuch, having bought a boy, would dress him in fine clothes and feed him delicacies. His chef would later cook the boy and serve him to the eunuch, earning ten ounces of silver per boy for keeping this arrangement strictly secret. Each time he had to kill a boy, the chef would chase them around with a cleaver, and all the boys would weep and cry as they fled before him. The chef would wait until the boys had worked up a sweat and excited their *qi*, then he would select the fattest boy and cook him.

One twelve-year-old knelt before the chef in tears and kowtowed as he begged for his life. The chef was himself moved to tears, but he told the boy: "How can I save you? There's nothing I can do. You're trapped here."

Just then, a messenger came in to announce that a certain local official had come to pay a call on the eunuch.

"It's fated that I should let you escape," the chef told the boy. "A local official is out there meeting with the eunuch. Grab onto his robe, wail piteously, and beg him to save you. If he's willing to take you with him, then you'll live and I'll die in your place. You can then spread the word that people must never, for any reason, sell their sons into the eunuch's mansion."

The child raced over to the official and wailed that the cook was trying to kill him. The eunuch immediately ordered his chef apprehended and beheaded, furious that he had released the boy. With a smile on his face, Gao ordered the boy back into the house. The boy, however, kept a death grip on the official's garments and begged him to save him. The official suspected that something must be amiss, so he took the boy with him when he left. The boy told him about all the others who had been killed in the eunuch's residence, making the official gasp in astonishment. But, considering that he had not personally seen any evidence that the eunuch had really bought the boys, and lacking testimony from the cook, the official didn't dare adopt the boy himself. Instead he took the boy to another region and found him a foster home. Later, the boy became an itinerant beggar and drifted around the vicinity of Fujian's Jianning prefecture. When people asked him about the eunuch's mansion he told them of riches beyond human imagining. Only when people learned of the eunuch's cannibalism were they dissuaded from selling him their sons.

A few years ago, Eunuch Gao was executed for his crimes, and hundreds of parents who had sold him their sons waited for them by the roadside. Not a single one appeared, however, and they all shed bitter tears that their sons must have been victims of the depraved eunuch's cannibalism.

Destitute people who sell their sons are fools! If their livelihood is insufficient for raising a son, why not beg in father-son teams, as they do in Fengyang prefecture?[1] That way, the parents could protect their flesh and blood. Should doing so truly be impossible, the only other recourse would be to sell the son into servitude in a wealthy household. By no means should they serve him up as a tasty morsel to a eunuch. Selling a son to a chapel or temple as a servant or attendant is equally unacceptable. Doing so would reduce one's son to a level below that of a beggar. The State[2] employs eunuchs for the sole purpose of keeping the palace in order and transmitting imperial orders, yet eunuchs wield power and exact profits, wallow in hedonism, and—worst of all—attempt to regrow their organ in order to defile women. (Some succeed, some don't.) Even if their cannibalism could be considered analogous to "wanting to mend one's decrepit body," did they not already accept that it was their fate not to be whole? Such outrageous behavior is utterly intolerable. Mencius says: "He keenest for battle deserves the severest punishment"[3]—and the eunuchs too engage in conscription and slaughter. They treat human life as worthless, and for no good reason. If the law of the land is to shine forth, such eunuchs must not be allowed to go on living.

Notes

1. Taking Fengtang 鳳湯 as a miswriting of Fengyang 鳳陽, a prefecture in South Zhili.
2. A blank space appears in the original text before the word State (*guojia* 國家); this was a standard typographical expression of respect for imperial institutions.
3. *Mencius*, 4A.14.

Type 20

Corruption in Education

Pretending to Present Silver to an Education Commissioner

Whenever education commissioners go on inspection tours, crooks follow in droves. Their marks are the sons of the rich who are seeking an in with the examiner. They beguile these aspirants with innumerable schemes promising success in the exams, but these always turn out to be scams. Should no one be buying one scheme, the next bunch will come up with a new way to fleece their victims. As a result, people fall for their tricks year in and year out. And since the families are too embarrassed to report it, people keep getting taken in.

There once was an education commissioner who was extremely fair in his adjudication of examinations and would not accept any inducements. A crook came along claiming he could get to the commissioner, but no one believed him. The crook's explanation was as follows: "This commissioner secretly accepts direct bribes because he hates to let them pass through others' hands. You have to give it to him personally, but then it works like a charm—all it takes is guts! If you really want to do it, get the cash and I'll hand it to him in person—and then it's a sure thing."

"Where should one give it to him?" asked a certain Zhao Jia.[1]

"When he's leaving the school, I'll present a calling card introducing you: 'So-and-so, from Such-and-such County, with X amount of silver, asks to be selected for advancement.' If he nods approval, I'll give him the silver; if he doesn't, I'll still have the money in hand, so he can't touch me."

"I'll want to be there to see."

"Of course you can watch. When the inner gate of the school is open just an inch, you can see straight through to the school building from outside. You'll be able to peek in."

"If the commissioner will really take the money himself, I'll do it."

So Zhao wrote out a calling card and wrapped a package of two hundred ounces of silver in a kerchief. In the afternoon he waited in front of the school for the commissioner to come out. "I'll need that calling card and the 'entrance fee,'" the crook told him. Zhao handed them over. When the commissioner was about to leave the school, the crook pushed his way in with the silver and the calling card, having told Zhao, "As soon as the gate has closed, peek in through the opening."

As the commissioner emerged from the school building, Zhao looked through the opening and saw the commissioner, still in his gauze cap and collared jacket, making his way out. The crook rushed up to him and presented the calling card, which an attendant accepted. The commissioner opened it and read it, and then slipped it into his sleeve. The crook then held up the packet of silver. The commissioner cast a glance at another attendant, who accepted it, whereupon the commissioner turned around and went back inside, followed by the attendant with the money.

The crook raced back to the inner gate and said to Zhao on the other side, "It worked! It worked! It's a done deal. Did you see?"

"He really took it—I saw it with my own eyes."

"We can't leave the school grounds tonight, so we'll have to stay between the two gates."

"Since everything's set, I don't mind skipping dinner."

The next morning, they slipped out together when the gates were opened and went to Zhao's inn to celebrate. As Zhao treated him to a big banquet, the crook said, "Don't forget to thank me after you pass with honors."

"Of course I'll reward you, just as we agreed."

This is a warning against trusting crooks.

When the exam rankings were published, the student's name was not on the list, and the crook was nowhere to be found. Zhao then realized that the whole procedure for offering the bribe had been a set piece created by the crook and a yamen underling who dressed up as the commissioner. Looking in from the inner gate to the school entrance, he could see the exchange with his own eyes—but only at a distance. He could hardly be sure of what was really going on, and so he fell for the swindle unawares. Had it been the real commissioner taking a bribe, would he have done so in his official robe and cap? Would he have taken the calling card at the entrance to the school, and accepted the money there too? Why on earth wouldn't he have received the calling card in private? Furthermore, the commissioner's subordinates lived in the school, so it was hardly a sufficiently private place to accept a bribe. This rich rustic knew nothing about how officialdom works, so he just trusted what he saw with his own eyes. Little did he know that what appears before your eyes is precisely what has been put there to deceive you.

Note

1. Jia 甲 is not a real name: it is the first item in the counting system called Heavenly Stems (Tiangan 天干). The Stems are often used as placeholders, for example in the names of people in hypothetical legal cases and in algebra problems. An English approximation would be "Zhao A."

Affixing Seals in a
Functionary's Chambers

When Qian the First, a wealthy man, sought to buy an examination degree for his son, his agent Sun Bing set out to swindle him. "An official surnamed Li, from our town, is a former colleague of the education intendant, and the two are very close." Sun told Qian. "He need only say a name for the candidate to be guaranteed a pass. Shall I discuss your case with him?" "Sure!" Qian agreed.

Sun Bing went to an artisan's stall, where he spotted two identical hanging crates. He bought one for three tenths of an ounce of silver and put down a deposit of two hundredths of an ounce of silver for the second, telling the artisan: "I'll send someone else soon with another three tenths of an ounce for this one—just don't switch it for another."

He also bought two identical locks, and then brought the crate and one of the locks to a servant in the household of Li, the local official, telling him, "Weigh out two hundred ounces of rocks and store them in this crate, lock it with this lock, and keep it in your master's chambers. In a little while I'll bring a fellow by who'll ask to have the old man put in a word for someone on the exam. He'll give you two hundred ounces of fine silver to put a seal on. Take the crate with the silver and give him back the one with the rocks. Later we can split the silver fifty-fifty."

"Okay," Li's servant agreed.

Sun Bing had the servant arrive to tell Qian the First, "I've met with Venerable Li, and he says this should be easy. Just have his servant watch you measure out the silver and lock it up, then deliver it to his residence, where they'll put a seal on it. They'll then send the crate back to you but hold on to the key. Once your son has passed the exam, make payment by sending the silver back in the unopened crate."

"I'll borrow a crate from you, then," Qian said.

Sun Bing said, "I've got a brand-new lock, but I'll have to go around the corner to buy a crate." He sent one of Qian's servants to the stall with three tenths of an ounce of silver to buy the crate. Qian the First, Li's servant, and Sun Bing all doubled-checked the two hundred ounces of silver, then Qian put it into the crate and locked it up. Sun Bing took the silver to the Li residence, along with Qian the First, to have the seal affixed.

Li was home sick, sitting in the chamber to the left of the main reception room. His servant carried the crate through the doorway and said, "We've already checked the silver, so we just need a seal."

Li replied, "Since you've checked it, he can take it back with him. Come get the seal."

The servant brought forward the crate of silver and all three parties affixed their seals. Qian the First removed the key and handed it to Li's servant.

Sun Bing then took the crate back to Qian's lodgings for him to keep. He said the whole thing had gone very smoothly.

When the examination results were announced, Qian's son's name was not on the list. Sun Bing said, "This business didn't work out, but you've still got the silver. You should take it back home quickly before Li's servant comes asking you to pay his transport costs."

Frustrated, Qian hurried off. Halfway home, he hired an artisan to open the lock, only to find that the crate was filled with rocks. Shocked, he went back to town.

"What kind of swindle did you pull on me?!" he roared at the go-between.

"I did everything in your presence," Sun Bing replied. "At what point could I have swindled you? Since all three of us sealed the crate, aren't the Lis just as much to blame? In any case, you've been gone for half a day and you opened the crate yourself; how do I know whether it was really silver or rocks in there?"

Qian realized that Sun and Li had colluded to swindle him, but he had no proof and it would have been impossible to get restitution. All he could do was curse the go-between and head home.

This is a warning against trusting local officials.

The two crates were identical, so one could hardly tell them apart. But the sealing of the crate should have taken place in plain sight; what need was there to bring it in first, then ask to have it sealed? And if at that point one did report it, and one were to track down the stall that sold the crate and ask why the two were identical, one might be able to prove that Sun Bing had bought one in advance and sent someone to buy the other later. Only the most brilliant official would have a chance of cracking this switcheroo swindle.

Silver with Sham Seals Is Switched for Bricks

In the prefecture of Jianning there was a man named Hao Tian-guang, who came from a very well-to-do family. They had several estates, most of which produced white rice. Once, the price of rice plunged in Jianning, but his business manager, Luo the Fifth, heard that in the provincial capital its price had skyrocketed. He and his boss thus decided to set off in that direction with two attendants and ten-odd boatloads of rice.

At the time, His Eminence Venerable Wang had just issued an order to hold an examination for candidates in the adjoining prefectures of Jianning and Yanping. Announcements were posted in both prefectures that Confucian Apprentices were to be tested.[1]

Just as the last of the rice was being loaded, a traveler with two attendants heading for the provincial capital boarded Hao's boat. As they were sitting idly during the boat ride, Hao Tianguang asked the purpose of his trip.

"I'm in charge of anonymized records for Venerable Wang," answered the man, who implied that he might have a certain influence.[2] Since Hao's eldest son was taking the exam, this piqued his interest. However, in the previous round of exams His Eminence had been extremely fair and immune to bribes, so Hao was not inclined to believe it could be done.

When they reached the provincial capital, the crook took his leave, saying, "When your son's exam comes before Venerable Wang, we'll be sure to look at it together, and I'll feel him out about what we've discussed, sir. Should he agree, I'll be back in touch so that we can reach an understanding. If you hear nothing, that means there's no chance of doing anything."

Although he still didn't trust the man, Hao said, "Sure." He sent one of his servants to tail the crook, who did in fact go into the examination grounds.

A few days later the man came back and told Hao, "It's doable. We just need to count out the silver. We'll keep it under seal in this leather case of mine. I'll let you hold on to the silver until the results are announced, then you can hand the case over to me." Hao thought to himself: *Even if we're counting out the silver together, so long as I keep it myself, what could go wrong?* So he did as the man suggested and they counted it all out.

Little did he know that this crook had an ingenious trick up his sleeve. Hao Tianguang put the silver in the case and locked it himself; all the crook did was attach a strip of paper to seal it up. As he left, he advised Hao: "Your son should be able to slip out of the exam grounds tonight, and I'll present him to the examiner. Then you'll be all set."[3]

Hao waited several nights in a row but heard nothing. Eventually, Hao opened up the leather case to find nothing inside but bricks and stones—the silver had all been nicked.

This is a warning against letting silver be swapped out from sealed containers.

Purchases of positions in government schools, of vacant offices, and even of provincial degrees—such things happen everywhere, every year. The prefecture of Jianning especially is overrun with swindlers and constantly suffers their baleful effects. No doubt this is because its residents are as wealthy as they are shallow and gullible. Despite having been the victim of multiple swindles, they try to purchase advantages again and again. For this particular itinerant crook, Jianning examinees were reliable marks. As for his technique for sealing up silver, even today no one has figured it out: he seals the silver while you watch and then gives it to you for safekeeping, but after he's long gone you open it up to discover nothing but rocks and bricks. Some claim it's a spell for making silver disappear, like magic! It dupes even the cleverest. So the lesson is clear: trust no one. If you really want to buy scholastic advancement, sealing up silver in advance is not the way to go. Instead, wait until your name appears on the official roster before making any payment; don't believe claims to inside information about who's passed. It may take three or four trips, but you want to see the final roster before handing over any money. That's the only way to avoid being taken.

Notes

1. The title translated as "Eminence," *zongzhu* 宗主, is not identifiable as a standard term for any position in the examination hierarchy. It could refer to the heir of a lineage, and in the Ming to a eunuch in the Directorate of Ceremonial, but neither sense is relevant here. Hence we have kept it as a vague term of respect for an official. Confucian Apprentices (*rusheng* 儒生) were students who had not yet qualified for positions in government schools.

2. Officials who assessed examination essays did so, in principle, without being able to tell who had written each exam. The essays were anonymized by replacing names with code numbers and by having scribes recopy each answer to preclude identification on the basis of handwriting.

3. During examinations, candidates remained locked inside the examination hall, separated from both the outside world and the examiners.

Robbed by a Gang While Sealing Silver in an Unoccupied Room

Swindles come in a wide variety, but competitors for advancement into the ranks of scholar-officialdom, being so numerous, are especially popular marks. There's a saying among crooks: "You can only make real profit off of false status, and you can only make real money off of false fame." Those who pursue advancement are so recklessly obsessed with status seeking that they'll throw away a fortune to make themselves a name. This is why they unthinkingly fall victim to the stratagems of crooks.

Once, the son of a rich family on his way to take the provincial examinations was on the lookout for a shortcut. He brought along his family's manager, an extremely capable man, and in the provincial capital they stayed with an agent, whom the scion engaged to seek out suitable connections. Over the next few days one prospective "way in" after another came by, but the manager, after observing their behavior and checking into their backgrounds, concluded that none lived up to their claims or had sufficient bona fides—and most were in collusion with the agent. Distrustful of their spurious promises, he rejected them all.

He then met a certain crook disguised as a simple errand runner who spoke in halting tones and behaved like a country bumpkin. The man claimed to be with a retired local official who was an old friend of His Eminence the examination chief and who had come to town to sponge off the latter. The "errand runner" brought the manager to see the man in question, who indeed had the look of an impoverished minor functionary.

They decided that for the promotion of a single examinee a donation of a hundred ounces of silver would suffice. The official's one condition was that the cash be sealed at his inn. "Let's seal it up at my inn," proposed the manager.

"This business requires the utmost discretion," said the retired official. "Your inn is crowded, and it would be most inconvenient if word were to get out. Down that way, however, are some unoccupied quarters—they were rented out to a certain *xiucai* named Gu who stayed until he found it too inconvenient to get supplies and moved back here. That would be the best place for you and my houseboy, Xiong, to conclude the arrangements."

The manager insisted that his inn was the proper place to seal the silver up, but the official said, "In case you have any doubts, from our side it will just be Xiong, and you can bring as many people as you want to help."

"No one else must know of this," the manager replied. "It'll be just me and my master."

When they arrived it was indeed just the errand runner, so they took out the silver to count it. Suddenly a group of bandits burst into the room and said, "Trying to buy a degree, are you? Well, we're turning you in!"

With that, they beat up the three men and stole all the silver. After they'd left, the errand runner pulled himself to his knees, seemingly in a daze. The manager grasped his hand and said, "No need to worry. It wasn't *that* much silver. Let's go back to our inn and prepare some more there."

But the errand boy refused to go, and the rich scion added, "The whole thing's a disaster. What's the point of trying again?"

"I've got an idea," replied the manager. "We just have to get the errand runner to come back."

He had the scion pack his bags and hurry home; meanwhile, presenting himself as a Confucian scholar, he had the errand runner clapped in irons and brought to the county office.

The manager reported that he had been robbed while purchasing a county-level degree. The magistrate said, "Your purchase of a degree was illegal, and both buyer and seller are guilty of a crime. Moreover, if some bandits robbed you of your silver, what's that got to do with that local official?"

"The ones who stole the silver were confederates of this crook," the manager replied. "If I could just track them down along with the silver, I'd happily forfeit it to the court. Furthermore, I acknowledge my guilt and will accept my punishment along with this crook."

The magistrate sent runners out to make inquiries, but the retired official was long gone. "He's a crook all right," the magistrate declared, and ordered a heavy flogging. The "errand runner" couldn't bear the torture and offered to pay back half the amount, but the manager told the magistrate that he was adamant about tracking down the others and willing to cover the travel costs. But the "errand runner," despite repeated torture, would rather have died than give up his confederates, so the trail went cold; he was ultimately sentenced to penal servitude. The manager was merely beaten and sent home.

This is a warning to guard against robbery when sealing silver.

The manager, capable as he was, still ended up being robbed by crooks. After the robbery, since he was able to capture the "errand runner" and was willing to share the culpability, he managed to recover half the amount, which prevented the crook from profiting from the scheme. Had it been the rich scion himself, surely he would not have been willing to share culpability, and the crook would have gotten off scot free. The question arises: if the manager was able to impersonate a Confucian scholar so successfully, shouldn't the officials have examined him instead of the scion? I would reply: those who negotiate bribes are worthless people to begin with, so it's not worth examining them. They could never pass, so it's no real loss.

A Fake Freeloader Takes Over a Con

Education Intendant Jian was a man of the utmost brilliance and integrity. Once when he was overseeing the provincial examinations, a freeloading acquaintance arrived from out of town and took up residence in the monks' quarters at Kaiming Temple.[1] The next day, a crook arrived with three servants in tow and took up lodging in the same temple.

Inside the temple, the crook introduced himself to the freeloader, saying that he too was a freeloader, come to sponge off his relative the local magistrate. Outside, his lavish dress and the retinue of servants following like bodyguards made for an impressive appearance. Examination students in the temple would notice his covered carriage going by and mistakenly say, "That's the friend of the education intendant from back home." On several occasions they also saw the genuine freeloader exchanging greetings with the intendant or going over for drinks. By shadowing him in this public fashion, the crook stole his identity and laid the groundwork for his scam.

Lord Jian was a strict and perceptive man, and within a few days the real sponger had been given a beating and sent packing. Now the only one left in the temple was the crook, who had his confederates spread the word outside that "the acquaintance of His Excellency the exam chief is in such-and-such a temple." Examination students shared this news with each other and many showed up seeking help to pass the exam. But they couldn't find anyone to leave the money with.[2]

The crook discreetly bribed the secretaries and clerks from the education intendant's office to make it known that packets of silver could be sent to their houses. This convinced everyone that the crook really was the intendant's freeloading acquaintance. If he was in cahoots with staff from the yamen and the silver packets were being sent to their house, what further concern could they have? The crook proposed to the staff that they set a quota of ten candidates who would each pay three hundred ounces.

When the candidates got to the examination grounds they vied for the ten spots, which were snapped up within a few days. The crook brought the candidates to the houses of the secretaries and, in broad daylight, deposited silver totaling three thousand ounces in packets that were carefully sealed.

Later, they secretly divvied the money up. The crook reflected that if the candidates didn't pass, he wouldn't be able to return the money. How to make a clean getaway? His solution was to pay someone to report to the intendant that he'd seen certain yamen secretaries colluding with a crook to recruit students, and that so many ounces of silver were being kept under seal in so-and-so's house.

Intendant Jian reported the situation to his superiors and issued an urgent bench warrant for the immediate arrest of the crook. By then, however, the phony freeloader had already made good his escape. Jian also apprehended the yamen secretaries, but even under torture from finger presses none would confess; each was given thirty blows and fired from his post. He also had the clerks' houses searched. Exam candidates who had been part of the conspiracy, upon hearing that it had been discovered, all fled back to their hometowns out of fear that they would be publicly identified and arrested. The silver they abandoned, being too afraid to try recovering it.

The crook thus was able to enjoy his share of the silver in safety. As for the secretaries, although they were fired, since there was no hard proof of corruption they all eventually wangled their way back in. They did have to endure beatings and torture—but because it was carried out by fellow clerks, it was all just playacting. So they came out ahead and lost very little.

This is a warning about the dangers of trusting spongers.

This crook pretended to be a relative of the Education Intendant. Exchanging courtesy visits with the intendant and sharing drinks with him would indeed have confirmed that they were related. And with secretaries constantly buzzing around him, who would have suspected that the man was a fraud? Unbeknownst to the exam hopefuls, the genuine relative had already left and a crook was usurping his identity. The yamen underlings, meanwhile, were just out for profit. With so much money at stake, they didn't mind suffering a few dozen blows; they still got their bit of the boodle, and while they lost their jobs there wasn't enough to convict them. Some folks nowadays claim that it's the clerks who know the law best. What they fail to realize is that it's the people who know the law best who are most wont to abuse it! Only through level-headedness, true accomplishment, and genuine learning can one earn a genuine reputation. Grasp not and scheme not, and you'll never be taken in by crooks' swindles. The lazy students and depraved fools who fell for this one brought disaster upon themselves.

Notes

1. The freeloader (*qiufengke* 秋風客) was a recognized social type, a hanger-on or sponger who takes advantage of a social or familial connection to a wealthy or powerful person in order to solicit money, lodging, food, or other benefits; he might also seek to bolster his own prestige or, as in this story, peddle influence. His close association with the "crook" (*gun*) is demonstrated by a set of puns linking them in scene 13 of the play *Peony Pavilion* (*Mudan ting* 牡丹亭, 1598). On this category

more generally, see Xin Yu 辛羽, "'Da qiufeng' xiaokao" "打秋風"小考, *Yaowen juezi* 咬文嚼字 7 (2012): 40–42, and Li Sha 李莎, "'Da qiufeng' yuyuan kaoshi" "打秋風"語源考釋, *Guangxi minzu xueyuan xuebao (zhehui kexue ban)* 廣西民族學院學報(哲学社會科學版) S2 (2001): 239–40.

2. That is, the bribe would be held in escrow by a trustworthy third party, to be paid out if the candidate were successful and returned if he did not pass.

Money Stashed with an Innkeeper
Is Burgled

Three crooks ganged up for a swindle that netted them three hundred ounces of silver. Instead of dividing the loot among them, however, they pooled their capital to set the stage for a joint swindling venture. Their minds were set on a major con. First they sent one of their number across Fujian province with seventy ounces of silver to purchase a property in a prefectural seat two days' journey from the provincial capital. This property housed an earthen strong room, and the crook converted the rooms facing the street into an inn. He then spent fifty ounces of silver to take a wife, also buying a maidservant and a domestic servant. The few dozen pieces of silver left over he spent on provisioning his new household.

Travelers were eager to stay at an inn run by such a prosperous-looking family, which had servants, food, and furnishings to spare. This prefectural seat was near the provincial capital. In years past, when the examiners were unable to hold exams in every neighboring prefecture, they would, to make their own travel more convenient, summon those examinees to the prefectural seat for joint examinations. Examinees from rich families looking for lodgings invariably chose to stay there.

The sixth month of 1612, when the examinations were to be held, was fast approaching, and students from two other prefectures had also been summoned to sit for the examinations.[1] Staying at the inn were three first-level degree holders, or *xiucai*, from the surrounding circuit of Jianning-Shaowu. All came from fabulously wealthy households.

One day, a traveling Confucian scholar, richly attired in immaculate new clothes, docked his boat outside the city and came to the inn. He asked the innkeeper in private: "Of the *xiucai* here for the examinations, do you happen to know of any from wealthy families?"

"Three such men are staying at my inn," the innkeeper replied. "Why do you ask?"

"I have an attractive proposition to discuss with them," the scholar replied.

"What proposition? Why don't you tell me?"

"You're not a scholar, so you wouldn't understand. I'd best discuss this with the *xiucai*."

The innkeeper went to the guest rooms and approached the three *xiucai*. "A gentleman is asking to speak with the richest *xiucai* sitting for the examinations. He says he has some attractive proposition to discuss, but when I asked for details he wouldn't tell me. Would one of you gentlemen be willing to find out what it is?"

Together, the three *xiucai* went to the innkeeper's quarters and bowed in greeting. "Reverend sir, we understand that you're looking for men of wealth. We, your juniors, are all from families of means. What is this proposition you speak of?"

"What would you gentlemen be willing to do for a guaranteed pass in the examinations?" the traveler asked.

"We're open to anything," they replied, "but what special connections do you have?"

"I can't do anything myself, and I don't have any special connections. But since you're open to anything, each of you should prepare one thousand ounces of silver and bring it to this inn. Once I've weighed and wrapped it I'll return it to you for safekeeping. The route to success will follow."

The three *xiucai* made plans to procure the money from home and reconvene at the inn to have it weighed. The scholar bade them farewell and departed. The three *xiucai* had someone follow him in secret, and the person returned to report that he had observed him get on a boat that carried only his family.

The three *xiucai* were delighted. "He's one of the chief examiner's men, for sure."

The innkeeper came over. "What was the proposition he told you about just now?"

"It's not a sure thing," they replied, "but if it succeeds there's a big tip in it for you."

Four days later, the three returned to the inn with the money. The scholar met them at the appointed time, and each *xiucai* reported that he had prepared the full amount.

"We'll check and seal up the silver tonight," the scholar told them. The *xiucai* told him that it would be inconvenient to carry so much money at night and suggested that they do it in the inner courtyard of the inn the next day.

"I'm afraid that the innkeeper won't keep mum. It would be more private to seal it up in an outer guest room," the scholar said.

"We'll see tomorrow," they replied, and the scholar took his leave.

After dinner, the innkeeper came to their rooms and said to them: "You all should be cautious in your financial dealings with this traveler. The doors and walls here are thin, so you'd better take precautions against him robbing you at night. If you take my advice, you'll store your money in my strong room. That way when you've retired to your rooms you can rest assured that you've taken prudent measures and that your property will be safe."

"You're right," they agreed. All told, they stashed six leather crates of silver in the innkeeper's quarters. Without telling his wife or servants, the head of the household then absconded with the money out the back door and fled with his gang of crooks in the dead of night. Before he left, the only thing he said to his wife was, "Tomorrow, if the three *xiucai* ask for me, tell them I went out early looking for someone and will be home soon."

The next day, the scholar arrived to weigh the silver with a big smile on his face.

"We left the money with the innkeeper for safekeeping. He went out early this morning and will be back soon," the *xiucai* told him.

The scholar waited until noontime with no sign of the innkeeper, so he took his leave and returned to his boat. That afternoon he sent someone from his family to inquire if the innkeeper had returned yet, but the answer was negative. At noon on the third day, the *xiucai* asked the innkeeper's wife to retrieve their leather chests, but she claimed she'd never seen any. And when they went to the stream to look for the traveling scholar, his boat was gone. Again they asked the innkeeper's wife for their money back, but she firmly insisted that she hadn't seen it. They forced their way in and searched the place, but no trace of it was to be found.

"Where's he gone?" they asked.

"He left two nights ago, and instructed me to say what I already told you."

Just as the three *xiucai* were panicking, the three crooks had crossed the border and made good their getaway, loot in hand. That night they put up at an inn. The innkeeper, noting that they had arrived late and were carrying six heavy chests, suspected that they were robbers or thieves, so he began recruiting people to apprehend them the next morning. The three crooks, catching wind of his plan, made off before dawn, taking just four chests with them and leaving the other two at the inn. The innkeeper became even more convinced that they were thieves and reported them to the local government office. The prefect had the seals broken, and inside one packet of silver discovered a contract stating that So-and-So had tried to purchase the title of Provincial Examination Graduate. The prefect summoned the government students named in the contract. At first they were unwilling to admit it, but after a little coaxing the prefect was able to hoodwink them into confessing and promptly threw them in jail. To be released, the *xiucai* had to bribe the prefect, who extorted another four hundred ounces of silver from them to block the referral of the case to his superiors.

The prefect also seized the innkeeper's house, sold off his wife and maidservant as state property, and sent the thousand ounces of silver from the two remaining chests to the treasury. The crooks who'd made off with the other four chests are fortunate that their names were never discovered, or they'd have been swindled by him as well. The prefect too was a crook.

This is a warning against trusting innkeepers.

Innkeepers with families are the most reliable, and anyone would trust a family man who offered to safeguard a traveler's money. Who would have imagined that this one's women were but purchased props on his swindling stage, whom he'd abandon once he had the profits in hand? Later on, this crook took other wives and concubines and enjoyed a life of wealth and status. If even innkeepers with families are not to be trusted, the world has become perilous indeed. Oh, why can't people stay level-headed enough to avoid being gulled by crooks!

Note

1. The text identifies the year as the *renzi* year on the sixty-year calendrical cycle, likely referring to 1612 but possibly to 1552.

Type 21

Monks and Priests

A Buddhist Monk Identifies a
Cow as His Mother

One summer, during the sixth month, an itinerant monk walking down a road came across a little boy leading a herd of oxen. Among them was a large, plump yellow cow. The cowherd stuck his left leg out for the cow to lick, which it did, and then he did the same with his right leg. "Why is that cow licking your leg?" the monk asked.

"She's the tamest," said the cowherd, "and I'm especially fond of her. She loves to lick my legs when they get sweaty and salty." From this the monk realized that the cow, which he secretly coveted, liked licking salty things.

The cow belonged to a husbandman. The next day, the monk slathered himself in thick brine from his head and face down to his hands and feet. He found his way to the house of the husbandman and knelt at the door crying, "I implore you to show mercy on my grieving heart and save my mother!"

"I've never practiced Buddhism or recited scriptures," the husbandman said. "How could I save anyone?"[1]

"When my late mother was alive," replied the monk, "she wouldn't follow a vegetarian diet or perform acts of virtue. Seven years ago, after she died, I was certain that she would be sent to the underworld as punishment for her sins, but my family was too poor to perform rituals or sutra recitations on her behalf. So I followed the example of Mulian saving his mother and voluntarily shaved my head and took on a master,[2] and have devoted myself to her salvation ever since. Last month I met a skilled fortune-teller who told me she was in your household, reborn as a yellow cow. I have come to respectfully ask to save her."

"There are four head of cattle in my barn. Would you be able to tell which one she is?"

"Let me take a look at them. All creatures have a spirit, and when mother and son meet there's bound to be a feeling of love that sets her apart from the others."

The husbandman took the monk to the barn and let the cattle out. When the monk saw the yellow cow, he opened his collar and removed his cap, then began to weep and knelt facing it.

"Mother!" he cried.

The cow smelled the salt and began to lick him all over his head and face, seemingly out of genuine affection. The monk cried even more and undid his robe; the cow licked him all over, unwilling to leave. The husbandman was astounded by the sight—it really did look like a mother who was unable to speak doting on her son. He asked the monk, "If this cow really was your mother in its former life, what do you need to do to save her?"

"If I had any money I'd gladly buy her at half market price and take care of her. But I'm a poor monk with nothing to my name but a robe and an alms bowl. If you'd be willing to give her to me, I would take her to my mountain chapel, where I could collect grass and prepare gruel for her every day until her sins are completely expiated. I'd care for her until her allotted years come to an end, and then I'd recite scriptures so that she can be reincarnated as a human being rather than a beast of burden."

"She's yours," the husbandman said, moved by this heartfelt speech.

The monk kowtowed his thanks and led the cow away to his mountain chapel, where they arrived after three days' journey. There he looked after the cow until the chill of the tenth month set in. Then he hired a butcher to slaughter it and sell half of the meat, which netted him an ounce and a half of silver. The other half the monk made into jerky, which he kept in his robe during his travels.

His wanderings eventually took him to the house of a powerful man. He entered the main hall and sat there cross-legged until the man came out and asked, "Monk, what are you doing sitting in my hall?"

"Don't you recognize me?"

"Why should I? I have no idea who you are."

"Doesn't my face look even a little familiar?"

"How could it? I've never seen you before."

The monk gave a long sigh. "All the liveliness of your spirit has been exhausted; no wonder you don't even recognize the face of an old friend."

"How could you be an old friend?"

"Back when Foyin enlightened Su Shi, or when Master Yuan called back Bai Juyi, weren't they old friends of Su and Bai?[3] In your previous life, you and I were devout practitioners, but because you did not fully separate your mind from the world you've come back to enjoy life in the human realm. I'm here to save you. In order to avoid losing the accumulated merit from your previous life, you must immediately clear your karmic debt from this world by returning to devout self-cultivation."

"How can you know about previous lives?"

"I have twice the accumulated merit you do. You've already enjoyed half a lifetime; I want to add another half lifetime of strenuous practice. After that, understanding past, present, and future lives will be easy."

"What devotions have you been practicing in this life?"

"I'll say no more about my previous lives for the moment. In this lifetime I've been fasting for the past three years."

"Well then, could you fast here in my house for a month?" asked the man, astonished.

The monk smiled. "It's already been three years—what's one more month!"

"Do you drink tea or water?"

"Clear tea or hot water, one pitcher a day."

The man agreed and swept out an empty room for him to sit in. Each morning he brought in a pot of tea, and each night one pot of boiled water. After seven days he invited the monk to come out, and they conversed normally. The man thought this so remarkable that he was convinced. "What sort of practice should I engage in?" he asked.

"Just give up your property and secular life and the right form of practice will be obvious."

"My wife would become a widow and my children orphans; to whom could I entrust my estate? I can't do this; what's the next-best form of practice?"

"Only by making donations to support temples and promote worship of the Buddha will you be rewarded in the next life. On Mount Lu is a hermitage that a lone monk is building all by himself. With a donation of five hundred ounces of silver he could complete it—that would bring you great merit."

The man agreed, sending a servant to accompany the monk with the silver and to stay for several days to gather information and report back. Later the monk took half of the silver and left.

His supposed "fasting" that convinced the rich man? He was eating the beef jerky. If only there really were people who could live without food!

This monk's theft of the cow was a relatively minor offense; turning around and selling it was no big deal. But for him to claim it was his reincarnated mother and then to butcher and eat it was a crime that reaches all the way up to Heaven. Using the jerky to feign fasting was an even greater swindle. Giving half the money to a chapel was a good thing, so this monk might have had some benevolent motives, but the money ought to have been shared with the less fortunate—why give it all to a chapel? This is the error of those fools who expect to reap rewards from the "field of benevolence."[4] *They must never have read Fu Yi's* Record of Lofty Knowledge.[5]

Notes

1. According to Buddhist theology, the fate after death of a human or other being depended on its actions in life: those who behaved morally would be rewarded with reincarnation in a desirable form (as a human in this world, or, even better, in paradise) while those who behaved immorally would suffer as an animal or, worse, as a tortured spirit in one of many hells. People could, however, influence not only their own fate (karma) but also that of others, by means of good deeds and religious rituals on others' behalf. This included the individual study and recitation of Buddhist scriptures (sutras) and the performance of rites by Buddhist monks.

2. In a popular story, retold in many folktales and operas, the monk Mulian descends into the underworld to save his sinful mother. The initiation of Buddhist monks included shaving off one's hair as a sign of renunciation of the world and one's body; this was one of the most visible indications of membership in the Buddhist clergy.

3. Su Shi 蘇軾 (1037–1101) was a famous poet, artist, and government official; he was a friend of the Chan (Zen) monk Foyin 佛印 (1032–98). Their friendship, and various means by which Foyin tried to bring Su closer to enlightenment, are the subject of several poems by Su and many later anecdotes. Bai Juyi 白居易 (772–846) was a renowned poet; the famous monk Huiyuan 慧遠 (334–416) is paired (under the name "Master Yuan") with Foyin in one of Su's poems, but given that Huiyuan lived centuries before Bai, either the name refers to someone else or the writer is misinformed about their chronology.

4. The "field of benevolence" is the Buddhist idea that support for charitable causes (such as donations to temples, road building, feeding the poor, etc.) brings karmic rewards to the giver.

5. *Gaoshi zhuan* 高識傳 (Record of lofty knowledge) is a collection of anti-Buddhist essays compiled by Fu Yi 傅奕 (555–639).

Eating Human Fetuses to Fake Fasting

There once was a Buddhist monk who claimed to be able to live without eating. Many rich families summoned him to test his abilities and observed that over the course of a week or so not one grain would pass his lips; every two or three days he would merely take a single bowl of boiled water. His renown grew such that people would vie for his attention by offering him money and silks.

A certain local official had an audience with the county magistrate, surnamed Chu, and the topic of this monk happened to come up. A monk of such lofty attainments existing in the mortal realm, he said, must be the genuine reincarnation of an immortal or a buddha.

Magistrate Chu, a man of strong and upstanding character, was distrustful of Buddhists and Daoists. "Can the material body with which man is endowed survive if he foreswears material nourishment? These fake fasters simply hide dried goods on their person to dupe common fools! How could an enlightened gentlemen believe such a fraud? If he were really able to live a life of fasting, he would keep himself hidden away deep in the mountains. His concern would be to avoid fame—what on earth would he be doing wandering the villages and markets? And just what use would people's silver and silks be to him?"

This reproach made the local official feel like he was being accused of heterodoxy, and he became even more determined to persuade Magistrate Chu to believe him.

"If you don't believe it, my lord," he replied, "you should summon the man here and test him yourself. That'll convince you that what I've told you is wholly legitimate."

Magistrate Chu promptly set a runner out to bring the monk in. He ordered a body search and forbade the monk from bringing in anything other than a string of twenty-four prayer beads. He then had him ushered into a clean-swept room and seated on a cloth mat. He posted sentries to spy on the monk in shifts. By day, another servant would go in the room and observe the monk directly, locking the door behind him when he left. For two days, sure enough, the monk sat there with crossed legs and an unchanging countenance. On day three, they looked in on him and saw that he was sweating slightly. The monk requested some boiled water to drink, and Magistrate Chu ordered that it be given to him. After the water was delivered, the servant went out and locked the door, then spied on the monk from outside. He reported to the magistrate, "The monk added one of his prayer beads to the water, and, from the look on his face, he recovered after drinking it."

Thenceforth, the servant took in one bowl of boiled water every two days and each time he reported what he spied from the outside: "He's eating the beads."

After eleven days, Magistrate Chu had the monk brought out and saw that only nineteen of the prayer beads he had brought in were left. Chu confiscated the beads and gave orders that the monk be imprisoned under light guard and left undisturbed in order to observe him meditating and wait for his next move. Chu also secretly instructed the jailer, "Don't allow any Buddhist or Daoist clergy to visit him. In two days he is certain to beg you for food; at that point, ask him how he made the prayer beads he's been mixing with water. If you can make beads identical to his, I'll reward you handsomely."

The next day, the monk asked the jailer for food, and the jailer replied with a request: "Teach me how to make your prayer beads and I'll give you food."

"This medicine is nearly impossible to get hold of," the monk replied. "But if you feed me, when I get out I'll pay you a handsome reward. Just don't ask for the recipe."

The jailer refused to give him food, and in three more days the monk's complexion had taken on an inhuman pallor and he collapsed from hunger.

Magistrate Chu had him brought for interrogation. "I've known all along that these beads are made from human fetuses. Tell me the process for making them and I'll spare your life."

The monk, too afraid to answer, feigned being on the brink of death.

Magistrate Chu just laughed. "Take a good look at this fasting monk, everyone! Three days of fasting under Magistrate Chu's supervision and he's nearly starved to death! These pills are made from fetuses taken from a woman's womb. To make them, you must kill a pregnant woman and then extract the unborn child. Just how many lives have you taken in this evil enterprise of yours? You'd never dare say. And why would I bother to get your recipe? Death by beating would be too good for you."

With that, he ordered his subordinates to set up a platform on which he displayed the nineteen beads, four of which he used to demonstrate the preparation method to the populace. When he stirred them in boiling water, the liquid in the bowl turned into a viscous slurry. Those bold enough to taste it found it both sweet and fragrant. A mouthful was enough to keep one full for a day. Magistrate Chu distributed the remaining fifteen beads to doctors for use in treating invalids. He then had the monk bound on a platform and executed by slow slicing.

"The county magistrate is a parent to his people," Magistrate Chu declared, "and while he cannot bear to kill, he is doing this on their behalf to vent their indignation."

The people declared themselves satisfied, and the local official never again trusted Buddhists or Daoists.

Such fake fasters mainly eat concealed dried provisions; eating human fetuses is rare. They don't keep the food on their person for fear of being searched, instead having a mendicant carry it and deliver the food to them while they're being tested. Some eat pine needles or bamboo leaves, the former with sowthistle tasselflower and the latter with tender ferns, both of which are edible and go down easy. Buddhist monks have duped others by claiming to survive on such things. Although stories about people surviving without food have been told since ancient times, this practice comes from the land of the immortals and is not a feature of the human realm. Yet some have encountered marvelous persons who have passed on the secret of fasting. Here is one such story.

In a grotto in the Wuyi Mountains,[1] a poor commoner built himself a hut just large enough to accommodate a bed and a stove. He cleared the mountainside to plant tea, which he sold to feed himself. After a decade or more, his plantation had grown to the point where it brought in three or four ounces of silver a year. Day in and day out he labored tirelessly, resting only in times of extreme heat, cold, or stormy weather. Those days he would spend sitting alone in his grotto hut. He had neither knowledge of scriptures nor other people to keep him company.

Then one day a Daoist appeared by his hut and addressed him, saying, "You work so hard farming these mountains. Why don't you hire someone to operate your plantation for you? You could earn an ounce of silver a year to buy clothing, and I could teach you my fasting method, so that you wouldn't need to buy food. You could avoid the toil of mountain farming and enjoy an easy life."

The mountain man replied, "I've heard that there are practitioners of such fasting methods. If you'd be willing to instruct me, I'd gladly serve as your humble disciple."

The Daoist told him, "Your tranquil disposition is perfectly suited to the practice. From now on you need only do the following: every morning, boil two crocks of pure spring water until half of it has boiled off, then combine them into a single crock. Morning, noon, and night, drink two cups of this water. After drinking, purify your heart and empty your thoughts, press your tongue against your upper palate, close your mouth and your eyes, and spend the day in meditation. Should the weather be amenable and your spirit invigorated, you might wish to take a stroll. Should you do so, just maintain a slow pace and roam as your fancy leads you, taking in the scenery at your leisure. The important thing is that, be it morning, afternoon, or any other time of day, and no matter whether you are active or at rest, you should follow without resistance the guidance of your mind. Should you come across fruits or edible plants on the mountains, feel free to nibble on them. Just don't actively go seeking them out. This, then, is how to live a life of fasting. Remember it well, and do not lightly share it with others."

The mountain man followed the Daoist's instructions for one year and, sure enough, not a single grain passed his lips. His face took on a golden radiance, and he remained as spry and healthy as ever. His neighbors in the mountains never saw him buy rice, and those who passed by his hut noted the absence of pots and pans. When asked about this, the man told them, "This past year I learned a fasting method."

The remarkable news passed from one resident to another, and some sought out the man and asked him to teach his fasting method to them. But he evaded them all, explaining, "My master instructed me not to share it lightly."

By the following year, word had spread far and wide, and the mountain man was besieged with callers. One person even brought provisions and took up residence in his hut, but over a full month of watching all he saw the man do was drink boiled water and silently meditate. He did nothing else, not even engage in conversation. Some ignorant visitors would pester him with questions or speak to him about self-cultivation, but he would just smile and get up for a walk along the mountain paths, not returning until midday or evening, when he would reheat and drink his boiled water. He never greeted these visitors, never saw them off, and said not a word in response to their queries. When questioned about mundane matters he might offer a casual word or two, but when asked about anything beyond that he would shake his head and remain silent. When anyone tried to harass him, he would simply go off and meditate. In speech and action, he treated everyone with utter indifference.

Another year passed and the man's fame grew. Now many rich and noble personages would send sedan chairs to invite him to their residences; invariably, he would refuse these entreaties. Then these rich and noble personages began to come to press their invitation in person. When prevailed upon to travel to their residences, he would not touch a mouthful of their food but instead meditate in an empty room, as silent and immobile as a wooden buddha yet still able to speak and move.

After two and a half years, a rich man from Tanyang[2] extended the mountain man a courteous invitation, treating him with the solemn respect due to a supernatural being. On one occasion, the rich man plied his guest with tea and fruit, of which the man consumed a little. The host then prepared a light meal of tea and plain rice and earnestly entreated the man to eat. His guest strenuously refused, but was eventually prevailed upon to eat one bowl. Soon, the mountain man became ravenous. He took a bowl of boiled water, but it didn't quell his hunger and he requested more food. The rich man was happy to oblige him, and respectfully fed him. Over the following three days, the man had to eat five meals a day just to satisfy his hunger. In shock, the mountain man asked to return to the mountains at once. There, he drank water and meditated as before, but he was beset by hunger. Eventually, he had to resume eating three meals a day, just like normal people.

The Daoist this mountain man encountered was clearly an immortal, and if the mountain man had been able to fast a full three years he would certainly have achieved transcendence himself. What a pity that fame took such a toll! First it was invitations, then he was forced to eat, and in the end he squandered his earlier accomplishments. That stupid rich man who urged him to eat thought that by treating him with respect and devotion, some of the good fortune of this living buddha would rub off on him. Earnest devotion to the Dao indeed! As for the mountain man, though he did make a mistake, his good fortune remained unaffected. The rich man, however, by committing this major sin surely set himself up to be a sworn enemy of the mountain man in the next life. As I see it, fasting is a practice of the immortals that involves more than just drinking boiled water and meditating—otherwise, he could just have gone back to his regimen of drinking and sitting, once more avoiding all food. So those Buddhist and Daoist monks who purvey fasting methods while asking for money and food are out-and-out robbers and thieves. No one who really knew how to survive without eating would dare to share this knowledge with others.

Notes

1. The Wuyi range, located on the border of Fujian and Jiangxi provinces, was home to many Daoist and Buddhist temples and a center of tea cultivation.
2. Here, Tanyang seems to be a literary designation for Jianyang, Fujian.

Type 22
Alchemy

Trusting in Alchemy Harms
an Entire Family

Magicians have duped countless victims over the course of history with alchemical hoaxes. Only the most perceptive people are able to recognize their spuriousness and reject them as false.

There once was a Daoist surnamed Bing whose magic was extremely powerful. He was lame in one foot. He let out that he was the inheritor of a genuine alchemical method but was reluctant to refine metals for others. His trick was to let others use his alchemical elixir, and, whether they smelted it with copper or lead, the product would be silver. When he used the elixir himself he didn't even need to refine it, he would just pick something up and it would become silver. Encountering a destitute person, he would hold the elixir in his palm and, with a flick of the wrist, produce some silver for them. Or he would reach into his sleeve and bring out silver, a great deal of which he distributed to the poor. Hence he was known as the "semi-seraph."

One time, someone treated Bing to a lavish banquet on silver dishes. When the meal was over, Bing had a rice barrel brought in and placed on the mat. One by one he placed the silver dishes into the barrel, but when the host looked inside the barrel was empty. "I've removed your dishes, and they won't be coming back," he told his host. The host politely asked for their return. "They're back in your house, in the place where you usually store them," Bing told him. And when the man looked, sure enough, there they were.

Were someone to use unpleasant language to force him to give something back, however, it would be gone forever. The Pentademon Transport Spell, as it is known, was but one of his many strange and amazing powers.

A rich man named Yao Lu came to believe in Bing and had him stay in his home. Yao worshiped him day and night, extended every sort of ritual deference, and sought to learn his powers. The Daoist received all of this worship serenely but would not transmit his teachings. Every day he would sit there soaking up this veneration and then drink himself into a stupor, not taking any of this deference seriously. But he did have real powers: everyone who worshiped him became joyful converts, and, having shared a drink with him, would sing praises of his mastery of the Way.

Yao Lu's entire household, young and old, and even the maids and servants, revered the Daoist. Only Yao's wife, Ms. Xin, distrusted him from the start. Again and again, she urged her husband to stay away from this evil man. When Daoist Bing learned of this, he gave one of the household servants two tenths of an ounce of silver and said, "Next time your mistress combs her hair, take a strand of it from her comb and bring it to me." The next morning the servant brought him the hair, and the Daoist used it to cast a spell.

By mid-morning, Ms. Xin's mind was focused on just one thing: intercourse with the Daoist. She told her maid, "Today I'm feeling a little odd inside."[1] By noon the feeling had intensified, and she repeated, "I'm really feeling quite odd inside." By mid-afternoon, she couldn't restrain her feelings and blurted out to her maid, "Until now I've loathed Daoist Bing, but today for whatever reason I'm infatuated with him. Tell me, how does my face look?"

"You look like you're falling asleep," said the maid.

After dinner that night, Ms. Xin was lusting after the Daoist, and the only thing holding her back was the presence of the rest of her family. Holding herself together with great effort, she whispered to her maid, "From now on, you must stay close by my side. If you see me going into the Daoist's room, slap me twice, right on the cheek. Don't forget!"

By the time she went to bed, her husband was already asleep. Ms. Wei undid her robe, revealing her naked nether regions, opened the door, and rushed over to the room of the Daoist, who just then was drawing her in with a magic talisman. The maid ran after her, shouting, "That's the Daoist's room, don't go in there!"—but Ms. Xin did not respond.

"Go outside," the Daoist told the maid, pulling Ms. Xin in by the hand. The maid advanced and gave her mistress two slaps on the cheek, to no effect, and then twice more on the face, saying, "You're not dressed!"

Ms. Xin finally began to come to.

"I was just dreaming that I came here," she remarked. "How is it that I find myself here in the flesh? It's a good thing you roused me." Taking her maid by the hand, she said, "Quick, back to my quarters. How embarrassing!"

She went into her bedroom and kicked her husband awake. Then she gave him a detailed account of everything that had happened, up to when she'd be roused by her maid.

"How is that possible?" her husband replied. "You've always hated him, so you must have concocted the whole thing. How could you have had a mind to go, but also instructed the maid to restrain you? You're lying—I don't believe a word of it."

The next day, Ms. Xin had no option but to relate the whole story to her husband's elder brother. The brother told her husband to get rid of the Daoist, but Yao wouldn't, so the brother reported it to the county court. The magistrate had the Daoist brought in and given twenty strokes of the rod, but he was able to take the blows with no pain at all, so the magistrate threw him in jail. The Daoist went into prison with nothing, but from his hands he produced silver. This he used to bribe the guards, having them buy wine and meat and bring it to his cell. The guards practically worshiped him, in hopes of learning his secret. He was subsequently acquitted by the prefectural and circuit courts, as officials tried to lay additional charges that all had to be dropped for lack of evidence. Finally, he paid a bribe and escaped, and his whereabouts are currently unknown.

A succession of Yao Lu's family members from different generations ended up dying of illness, poisoned by the Daoist's witchcraft. Only the chaste and upright Ms. Xin enjoyed a long and healthy life, managing household affairs and raising her children and grandchildren. She lived to over ninety.

Dark sorcery beguiles like a fox spirit: it can lead astray only a mind that already has some evil in it. Keep your mind upright, and even if evil spirits surround you they will not be able to harm you. That is why, when Fu Yi did not believe in the death hex, the barbarian monk who cast it himself died, and, when Zhongyan did not believe in the ghost that killed his son, the ghost simply did not haunt him.[2] Since Ms. Xin's mind was upright, even when confused by devilish magic she was able to give advance instructions to her maid and avoided being poisoned by its evil. Indeed, even the most ingenious magic cannot overcome genuine rectitude. So should you ever encounter such witchcraft, fortify your mind and pay it no heed; then the evil will have no way in!

Notes

1. Literally, she felt odd in her *xin* 心, anatomically the heart but also considered the seat of thought and emotions, hence sometimes translated as "mind-and-heart" or, as in this story, simply "mind" or "inside."
2. Both references are anecdotes about skeptics overcoming sorcerers. In the Zhenguan period (627–649) of the Tang dynasty, a foreign monk came to court and claimed to be able to kill people—and bring them back to

life—with a magic spell. The courtier Fu Yi, a vehement anti-Buddhist, rejected the claim and allowed the spell to be tried on him. Not only did it fail, soon afterward the monk keeled over and died. See Li Fang et al., *Taiping guangji, juan* 285. Zhongyan was the *zi* of Fu Yi's contemporary, Wang Tong 王通 (584–617); we have not identified the source of this anecdote.

A Foiled Alchemy Scam Leads
to a Poisoning

Ding Yuhong, a young fellow from Gutan, was a master of clever ruses. He had an unerring nose for imposture and was impossible to cheat. On one occasion he encountered a sorcerer who claimed to be an alchemist. Yuhong could tell at a glance that the man was a fraud and decided to swindle him. Playing dumb, he plied the sorcerer with all sorts of questions about his methods.

The sorcerer told him, "Alchemy is a supernatural practice that since antiquity has been passed down to men of virtue, expressly to relieve the suffering of the indigent. The first step is to select the chemicals to be decocted into an elixir.[1] Boiling a tenth of an ounce of silver with the elixir yields three tenths of an ounce of silver— you can turn one ounce of silver into three."

"Can you make even more than that?" Yuhong asked.

"So long as you have the elixir, you can make a hundred ounces, or even a thousand."

Yuhong gave him a tenth of an ounce to decoct first. The sorcerer added three parts elixir and boiled it into three tenths of an ounce of silver. Yuhong was delighted, and gave him an additional ounce to boil, yielding three. Yuhong was beside himself and invited the sorcerer back to his house, where he waited on him attentively. He gave the man all of the silver he had and asked him to create some more from it. The alchemist went on to produce another thirty-odd ounces of silver. Yuhong plied him continually with ingratiating questions about his methods. But instead of fronting any more money for alchemy, he ended up swindling away all of the sorcerer's capital.

The sorcerer figured that he couldn't very well deal with Yuhong in his own home, so he told him, "My elixir's all used up. If you bring more silver, I can go get more ingredients and we can head elsewhere to do wholesale alchemy."

Yuhong was well aware that the man wanted to lure him onto the road, the better to swindle him, but he thought to himself, *So long as I stay on my guard, he won't be able to get the better of me.* Eager to clean out the alchemist's remaining funds, he brought along fifty ounces of silver and left with him. He refused, however, to pay for any expenses. When the sorcerer asked for money to buy ingredients, Yuhong said, "Since you can turn elixir into silver, why be stingy with the silver you've already made? Just decoct some more for traveling expenses and I'll hold on to my silver to buy the ingredients later."

The sorcerer took out his three remaining ounces of elixir and Yuhong put in ten ounces of silver to make another thirty, which they divided evenly between them. They traveled a great distance over the next two days, and Yuhong remained vigilant even when he ate and slept. Unable to rob him, the sorcerer secretly bought some arsenic and hid it on his person. That night he bought a fresh fish and took it to their inn, where Yuhong cooked it and divided it into two bowls. As the sorcerer carried the first bowl over to where they were sitting, he slipped the poison into it. As he carried the second bowl over, he intentionally sneezed on it, spraying the fish with mucus. "This bowl's contaminated," he said. "I'll eat from it."

By midnight Yuhong was suffering stomach pains, which continued into the next morning. The sorcerer went to a doctor to get a painkiller, but after taking the decoction Yuhong's pain just got worse. By noon, Yuhong's hair was disheveled, his lips were cracking, and the pain in his stomach was unbearable. Suspecting that the sorcerer had poisoned him, he begged him, "I only have fifty-five ounces of silver on me. If you can save my life, I'll give you half."

At this point, Yuhong couldn't even get out of bed. The sorcerer took Yuhong's silver and put it in his own bundle, then came over to the bed and handed Yuhong a packet of medicine.

"I'm a traveler who relieves folks of their silver, and now you come along, you devious fellow, and swindle fifty ounces from me. Now I'm only taking five more ounces than you took from me. Consider this an act of charity: I've given you the antidote, but whether you make it or not depends on whether you're fated to live or to die."

With that he took his bags and fled. Yuhong, in a panic, had the innkeeper prepare the drug, which someone recognized as the remedy for arsenic poisoning. After several doses, the pain subsided and then ceased. Yuhong sought further treatment nearby; it took him three days to recover fully. The sorcerer had stolen all his money, so he had to beg his way home.

No one knew better than Yuhong how to guard against alchemy scams. He was impervious to all manner of swindles and even managed to swindle the bogus alchemist out of almost all of his capital. In this, he was brilliant. In the end, however, he was cleaned out of all of the money he had gained, plus five ounces of silver besides, getting poisoned and nearly losing his life in the process. He was lucky to survive and beg his way home, suffering hardship and indignity along the way. Never trust in the alchemy of sorcerers!

Note

1. *Dantou* 丹頭, literally cinnabar, but also a generic term for medicines, pills, and powders, especially miraculous ones.

Type 23
Sorcery

Using Dream Sorcery to Rob a Family

Foxes rest in mountain caves during the daytime and come out at night to feed on the fruits of the forest. Once, one of them happened to absorb from among the plants the primal essence of Heaven and Earth and underwent a magical transformation. This fox gained the ability to transform into a beautiful woman and would seduce men and steal their *yang* essence to increase its own powers.

A Buddhist master caught this fox and cooked it. A monk from his temple asked for the heart, which he baked slowly and smoked with fine incense. The monk then built a thatched hut deep in the woods and placed the fox heart inside as an object of veneration. By day he would incant all manner of repentances and sutras for its salvation. Nighttime would bring a host of demons and bizarre phantoms who would howl, scream, moan, weep, cry, and shriek. These apparitions could even speak—sometimes in human language and sometimes in barbarous tongues. Contorting themselves into all manner of bizarre shapes, they wailed outside the hut with laments for the dead, making a chillingly desolate sound. Only the bravest of men would dare to remain there. The laments continued for seven days, then gradually diminished. The monk continued reading sutras, casting spells, and making food offerings day and night. After forty-nine days, he burned down the hut and took the fox heart back to the temple, where he burned incense and candles to it.

The night before he planned to visit someone, he would put the fox heart into an embroidered sack and place it over his own heart. Invariably, he would then dream of a woman guiding him to the person in question. When he visited the person the following day, they would be so astounded at already having just met the monk in a dream that they would accede to whatever request he might make.

This is just one of the methods Buddhist monks use to swindle through transformation.

Another story concerns a rich man named Yang Lao who had two married sons. Despite all of his accumulated wealth, Yang was a miser unwilling to tithe a single coin. One night he dreamed that two monks of high repute came to him begging for alms. Sure enough, the next day he was visited by two monks whose faces looked identical to those he'd seen in his dream.

"You've been too reckless in accumulating wealth and have made many people resentful," they told him. "We share with you a fate inherited from previous incarnations and have come here specially to help you to repent."

"How must I repent?" Yang asked credulously.

The monks replied, "First, your entire family must undertake a vegetarian fast for three days. Next, purchase fruits, cakes, and noodles, and sacrifice a pig, sheep, and ox to make up a meal that is half meat and half vegetarian. We will then perform magic and make entreaties on your behalf, and recite Buddhist sutras to absolve you of sins committed in previous lives. Once the prayers are completed your blessings will increase, your house will be purified, and you'll avoid an afterlife in Hell."

Yang did as they instructed, fasting and purchasing the food offerings.

On the third day two other monks arrived, and Yang retained them to assist with chanting sutras. When night fell one of the monks uttered incantations and burned talismans, then put a charm on Yang that made him jump about and yell. He put a sword in Yang's hand and pointed to his wife and sons, telling Yang, "Those are demons." Yang stabbed them all, then started chasing after his two daughters-in-law, who appealed to the monk for help. The monk pointed at Yang and yelled "Sit!" Yang immediately put up his sword, gnashed his teeth, and fell to the ground, unconscious.

The four monks came in and gang-raped the two daughters-in-law. They then bound the women with rope and stripped the house of its valuables, tying them into bundles on four carrying poles, and fled into the night.

The next day a neighbor came into the house and saw Yang lying sprawled out over his sword with his eyes wide open, speaking in a trance. The neighbor rushed out and called for everyone to come and look. A group of relations jostled their way inside, where Yang Lao was still going on about wanting to kill demons. The crowd came up and wrested the sword away from him.

"Yang Lao," they asked, calling him by name, "why did you do this?"

Gradually, Yang regained his senses. Someone repeated the question until he was finally able to answer: "I dreamed I saw a host of demons in my house and was slaughtering them. Then you woke me up."

Yang then went into the back room and saw that his wife and sons had all been killed.

"I remember killing three demons here," he wailed. "I also remember trying to kill two she-demons before a monk stopped me."

Going into the bedroom, he found his two daughters-in-law tied up on the bed and called a female neighbor over to go in and release them. His daughters-in-law told him that they'd been raped by monks who had taken all of the family's gold, silver, silk, and other valuables. Consumed by bitter hatred, the Yangs had the three corpses encoffined and dispatched people in all directions to pursue the monks. After two days with no sign of them, the search was called off.

Yang Lao was an avaricious man who had come by some of his wealth through immoral means. This is why he believed the monks' story and shivered in fright when they spoke of people's resentment. He retained them to do penance on his behalf due to his sense of shame. In first appearing in a dream and then using magic to effect their theft, these monks were using the same technique as the monk who projected himself into dreams using a fox heart. Though they appeared in the dream to be esteemed monks, they turned out to be bandit monks. One would have to be deluded to give more credence to nighttime dreams than to daytime actions. And one would have to be stupid to think that one can go through life doing no good deeds but then gain absolution through discipline and fasting. All too often nowadays people abandon benevolence and righteousness for cruelty, greed, and violence—yet these same people will feed monks, worship Buddha, and make shows of piety and repentance. They're trapped in the same old rut as Yang Lao! This story offers chilling proof of the old saying: never do evil, and never trust a monk.

Type 24
Pandering

A Father Searching for His Wastrel Son
Himself Falls Into Whoring

Zuo Dongxi was a rich man whose only son, Shaoshan, once[1] went to Nanjing on business, taking with him a thousand ounces of silver in capital. Upon arrival in Nanjing he took up with a prostitute called Moon Blossom in the house of Madame Mao. When Shaoshan had been gone for an entire year, Zuo made inquiries and learned that his son, having fallen into whoring and hedonism, had abandoned all thought of returning home. Zuo wrote letter after letter urging his son to come home. At first Shaoshan would write back with excuses about accounts that needed collecting, but eventually the replies stopped. When Zuo learned that Shaoshan had already squandered half of his capital, he became incensed and resolved to go find his son himself. Not wanting the journey to be a total loss, he brought with him goods worth three hundred ounces of silver and set off for Nanjing with a servant, Shi Lailu.

Long before they and their goods had arrived in the capital, someone tipped off Shaoshan: "Your father's coming here on a sales trip and will be looking for you."

Distressed by this news, Shaoshan hurriedly summoned Moon Blossom's "mother," Madame Mao, to discuss what to do. "My father's on his way here to persuade me to go home. If you can come up with a plan to lure him into whoring too, I'll be able to stay longer. Otherwise, I'll have to say my good-byes tonight."

"Just hide yourself inside and don't let him catch sight of you," Madame Mao told him. "I know how to handle this."

With that, she sent a servant to invite over Madame Xun, who presided over the girls in the front courtyard, and asked her to help set a cunning trap. Madame Xun agreed and left.

Zuo asked a fellow merchant sojourning in Nanjing where he could find Madame Mao's brothel and learned that his son was courting the proprietress's "daughter," Moon Blossom. He soon found his way to Madame Mao's place, intending to order his son home. Madame Mao herself came out and welcomed him with the utmost courtesy.

"It's taken me ten days to get to Nanjing, so could you please just call that good-for-nothing son of mine to show himself?" Zuo said to her.

Madame Mao's reply was deferential and courteous. "Ah, so you are the honorable father of Young Master Shaoshan? How fortunate your unworthy servant is to meet you! Your son did stay at my humble abode for two or three months, but I saw him off over a month ago."

She then called Moon Blossom out to meet Zuo.

"Pay your respects to the gentleman," she said, indicating Zuo, who did not acknowledge her bow. Madame Mao then ordered a banquet to be prepared.

"I came here to fetch my worthless son," Zuo told her, "not to inveigle a banquet out of you. Hurry up and tell him that we're going. Don't try to detain me with false courtesy."

"But he really did leave over a month ago," Moon Blossom put in. "He said he was going to collect some accounts and then return home. If he were actually here, we wouldn't dare to deceive you."

Zuo didn't believe it and was determined to hunt the boy down. Madame Mao told him, "Our humble dwelling has only a few rooms, which you are more than welcome to search. How could we possibly be hiding him here?"

Moon Blossom led Zuo to the inner chambers, which he searched thoroughly but fruitlessly.

"The broker told me he was here!" Zuo exploded. "Where have you hidden him? Don't lie to me! If my son doesn't turn up, that means you must have killed him, and I'll sue you before the magistrate. Find him or else!"

Moon Blossom reacted with shock. "We'd *never* do anything to harm our customers! Don't make false accusations, sir."

Zuo cursed them roundly and left. Just as he was storming through the courtyard, a girl at the window dumped out a basin of water, drenching him from head to toe.

"Who was that?!" he hollered.

"It was someone from the brothel," Lailu replied.

As Zuo was cursing and gesticulating at her door, an alarmed Madame Xun came out and asked what had happened. When she learned that one of her girls, Auspicious Cloud, had accidentally poured water on Zuo, she had her brought out and beaten with innumerable strokes of the rod. Auspicious Cloud begged for mercy, but Zuo turned a deaf ear.

Madame Xun then commanded the girl: "You will now fetch Master Zuo a new set of clothes, kowtow to beg his forgiveness, and keep him company here tonight to make it up to him. Otherwise, you'll be asking for trouble."

Auspicious Cloud completed a full kowtow and then led Zuo into her chamber, where she took out a new set of clothing for him to change into. She then kneeled before him. "People in my line of work fear nothing more than giving offense. I pray that in your boundless magnanimity you'll see fit to forgive this slave's crime."

Zuo replied, "It's not that I blame you, but I can't very well go out in wet clothes. Now that I have these new clothes, I'll be off. I'll have them returned tomorrow."

He gathered up his robe and rose to go, but she caught him. "Let me offer you a drink to apologize first. If you go now, Madame will take it out on me again."

"How could I impose?" Zuo asked. A banquet had already been laid out and, with Auspicious Cloud solicitously keeping him company, Zuo relaxed and enjoyed his wine. By evening he was ready to depart, but Auspicious Cloud entreated him to stay, telling him: "I've had no guests for a long time. If you don't stay tonight, I won't be able to show my face again. Just stay the night and Madame will be delighted and praise me for being able to retain a guest. Aren't I worth the money?"

They continued drinking until the second watch and then retired. Zuo thought that he'd end up paying for her services eventually, but he feigned disinterest and didn't touch her, waiting to see what she'd do.

Auspicious Cloud cuddled up and caressed him. "Sir! You're being a real Liuxia Hui—a pretty girl sits on your lap and you're completely unmoved.[2] Do you plan on going home empty-handed from Treasure Mountain? Besides, 'no one knows what happens in the dark': they're not going to praise you for playing the chaste man tonight!"

Dongxi laughed and followed her lead. The next day, by the time he arose and did his toilette it was nearly noon. A banquet was already waiting, and Auspicious Cloud urged more and more drink on him, playing music and singing to keep him company.

As evening approached Zuo again wanted to be off, but Auspicious Cloud entreated him, "If you're willing to stay another night, Madame will be so happy. But if you leave after only one night, this will have been just a casual encounter—'a falling petal full of feeling, swept away by a heartless current'! I know that I've failed to wait on you properly, but I've suffered such a long drought of guests—you won't leave me high and dry, will you?"

Zuo was persuaded to stay yet another night. The third day he insisted on leaving no matter what and asked for his old clothing back, to which Auspicious Cloud replied: "I've already ordered a servant to deliver it to your lodgings."

"Tomorrow I'll return the borrowed clothing I'm wearing," Zuo told her.

"My only fear is that you don't like it. And why don't you take a keepsake?"

She then pulled out a chest of trinkets, intending to select a gift. Zuo saw that the chest was filled with pearls, jades, and expensive knickknacks. Auspicious Cloud took out a fan pendant, saying, "I hope you'll accept this unworthy token of my regard—it's made of silver."

"I appreciate the sentiment, but why silver?"

"This pendant was given to me by the scion of an official from the Board of Rites; you can see his poetic name engraved on the side. All of Mr. Fan's gifts to me are made of silver. The hairpins and ornaments and the like I have to hold on to, so that if I receive him again and he asks for them, they'll be right there and he'll see that I haven't forgotten him. For this reason, I don't dare give them away to anyone else. This silver fan pendant, however, he gave me in return for a favor, so I'm willing to give it to you. It has my name cast into the side."

Zuo took the fan pendant and left. The next day, he remarked to Lailu, "This prostitute sure is in a difficult position, it seems to me. She makes one mistake in pouring out a basin of water and ends up having to make up for it by being such a painstaking hostess. I wouldn't take a thing from her, except that I'm worried she'd be upset if I refused. I'll give her four ounces of silver for the two nights I stayed and the four banquets I ate. In return for the silver fan pendant, I'll give her three hairpins. You can take them to her when you return this clothing—I'm not going there again."

But Lailu, as it turned out, had for the past two nights enjoyed the company of the maidservant Guiying, and the two had grown so affectionate that each couldn't do without the other. Just before Lailu had left, Guiying had told him, "If your master comes back, we'll be able to meet again," so Lailu wanted nothing more than for Zuo to resume whoring.

"The other day you went there empty-handed, but she still treated you so respectfully," Lailu reminded him. "If you take her the money and hairpins today yourself, even if you don't stay the night you could at least stay for a drink. Why not enjoy another meal on her?"

Zuo took his advice and went back to the brothel to present the silver and hairpins in person. Auspicious Cloud beamed as she received the gifts, which she took to show Madame Xun, boasting, "Master Zuo gave me four ounces of silver and three hairpins! He must have been really pleased with my services to have given me so many gifts."

Madame Xun too was thrilled and came out with a bow to thank Zuo.

"We shouldn't be accepting such lavish gifts, but given your considerate patronage we hope you'll enjoy yourself a few more days at our humble establishment."

Zuo made some insincere protest that he had to leave, but Auspicious Cloud pulled him into her chambers, where a banquet was already laid out.

"Another banquet!" Zuo said. "How can I ever repay you for going to so much trouble yet again?"

Auspicious Cloud replied, "The earlier banquets were just to apologize for my mistake. Today's can be deducted from the silver you just brought me."

"The money I've already given you can be used to repay past expenses," Zuo told her. "But if I'm going to be your patron, you'll have to count my expenses starting from today."

With that, he whored day and night, losing all track of time. Lailu was reunited with Guiying, and the two servants, beside themselves with joy, became even more attentive and obedient in their duties, ever anxious to please. Master and servant alike wallowed in pleasure and set aside all thoughts of leaving.

Zuo would occasionally remark to Lailu, "This should stop. We've wasted too much money."

Lailu would respond by persuading him as follows: "Men of wealth ought to spend their money on enjoying the pleasures of women. Here you are, the head of a great household, finally able to enjoy a few rare months of happiness. Even if you were to spend all of your money, you wouldn't have to worry about family members back home going hungry. Besides, a man of your age should enjoy himself while he can. Even if you live to a hundred, why live as a miser?"

Zuo was infatuated to begin with, and following Lailu's repeated inducements he never looked back. Before he knew it, half a year was gone, and with it three hundred ounces of his silver. Guiying would periodically ask Lailu for gifts of clothing and jewelry, and Lailu would beseech his master for the money. Zuo asked him, "How much have I spent? I have no idea. We'll have to have Madame Xun do the calculation and hold on to enough to pay our way home."

When their bill was totaled up, they had already spent over three hundred ounces of silver. Zuo liquidated his stock, but even this was not enough to pay his debts, much less to have any left over for traveling expenses.

Lailu suggested, "Your son has plenty of funds; you could borrow some from him."

"I'm not in a position to open my mouth," Zuo replied. "You go and find some tactful way to bring it up with him."

When Shaoshan learned that his father had spent all his money on prostitutes, he clapped his hands and laughed uproariously. He had Moon Blossom arrange a farewell banquet and invited his father and Auspicious Cloud. He then went home with his father, not saying a word about what had transpired. Zuo imagined that his encounter with Auspicious Cloud had come about thanks to the workings of fate, completely unaware that he had fallen into a well-laid trap.

A femme fatale can corrupt a man; a beautiful woman can topple a city. Since antiquity this has been a cause for regret. How can a man whose will has been bent like a caterpillar remain pure and unsullied? Zuo had not come seeking female company—his only desire was to fetch his son and go home. He was well aware that prostitutes have the power to bewitch and that their clients end up bankrupt, yet he ended up sinking even deeper into the mire than his son. Rare indeed is the man able to stay away from carnal pleasures and avoid addiction to sexual passion! As Confucius put it: "I have yet to encounter a man who is as fond of virtue as he is of sex." Even a worthy man, if he is cavalier about matters pertaining to sex, will find himself in trouble. That's why the saying in brothels is: "Don't worry that comers will be clever customers; just worry that customers will be too clever to come!" Only those who never set foot in the prostitute's domain can stay free of her snare. As for those who do take that step, none has avoided falling under her spell.

Notes

1. Reading *chang* 嘗 for *chang* 常.
2. Liuxia Hui 柳下惠 (720–621 B.C.E.), of the Kingdom of Lu, is regarded as a paragon of moral propriety for having kept his hands to himself when he had a woman sitting on his lap. In some versions of the story, he let her sit there throughout a cold winter night because he was worried she would freeze to death.

Appendix 1

Preface to *A New Book for Foiling Swindlers: Strange Tales from the Rivers and Lakes*

I have heard it said that eras of decline are rife with vice and thievery. Armies pillage to the east while bandits run riot in the west. Yet even for such threats there exist remedies, both offensive, like those of Lu Ban, and defensive, like those of Mo Di.[1] Hence the master of his times fears not the rushing torrent but remains a bulwark in the face of roiling waters. He does not disdain to learn from even the humble woodcutter; he also draws lessons from past failures, avoiding roads that once tipped the cart. Softer stones can be used to cut into jade, and the light of a candle on one's brow is enhanced by a basin of water.[2] Likewise, even medicines that do not extend life can replace rich fare as a means of attacking an ailment; puppets that can hardly defend against an assault may yet stand in for infantry in lifting a siege.[3] Even an ointment for chapped hands can help to defeat an enemy.[4] Excessive focus on minutiae, of course, is akin to trying to carve a monkey onto a thorn—such ingenuity cannot make good every deficiency.[5] In an age at the mercy of wind and waves, only a precious raft can assure safe passage.[6]

In these times far removed from antiquity, morals degenerate and fraud flourishes with every passing day. The crafty take advantage of the artless and the wise deceive the foolish. A person's glib tongue may well conceal the dagger in his heart. This one harbors deceit, that one suspicion—no human interaction nowadays can be heartfelt and candid. Demons and spirits haunt the world and phantasms sweep the heavens. Everyone is secretly armed, pitting mental pikes against shields of the will. Intrigues blanket the benighted earth, like imps spitting poison at shadows in the dust.[7] Still, bright sunshine can unmask mountain demons and a cunning rabbit may magically escape the snare.

As light turns swiftly to dark, all might well seem lost. Some curry favor by letting a deer be called a horse, while others arrogate the authority of the powerful like the fox walking before the tiger.[8] Some fraudulently claim to bear miraculous seals, while others perspicaciously dodge an awl hidden within a sack. Everyone falls over themselves in their struggle for victory through clever rhetoric, their subtlety and deceit making every place a battleground. Compared to this, the Qutang Gorges of the Yangzi were never so perilous and the treacherous cliffs of Mount Taihang present an easy path. You might possess greater acumen than the elite troops of Sun Zi and still lose twice for every victory won. Your cleverness might surpass that of the monkey master, yet you would not outdo his scheme of pleasing his charges by reversing their ration to four acorns in the evening and three in the morning.[9] Only the rhinoceros horn of Ji Huanzi was able to cast light on the river monster at Ox Islet, but even with the mirror of the Qin ruler it would be difficult to illuminate a heart in this dark sea.[10]

The decline in morals has reached such a crisis that a gentleman of conscience cannot help but be alarmed. Such a man is Master Zhang Yingyu of Jutan,[11] who is both wise and deeply concerned for the world's welfare. Lamenting the now-distant golden age of the Xia, he reflected long and hard on his own experiences. Having personally hazarded routes as dangerous as the Ninefold Slopes, seen through the false and the vulgar with his own eyes, and broken through the barrier of a hundred fears, he proceeded to research earlier accounts with meticulous care, hunting out examples near and far to create a book that captures the true state of the populace and the spirit of the age. All underhanded dealings he reveals as if he held them in the palm of his hand. Treacherous hearts and thieving ways he plucks from their hidden recesses and presents before our very eyes. Once a cataract has grown, only a metal needle can pierce it; when tricksters have arisen by the hundreds, only the power of the Law can wash them away.

Master Zhang's work is akin to that of Yu the Great, who cast into his Nine Cauldrons the form of every kind of animal, monster, human, and demon. So too is it like that of the Divine Farmer, who described all the medicinal plants and recorded their mild, cool, sweet, and bitter properties. Of old, the Duke of Zhou, troubled by the world's decline and worried about its precarious state, put his ideas into the explanations of lines in the *Book of Changes*.[12] Master Zhang also resembles Master Han Fei, who, reacting to the political machinations of his day, poured his anger into the chapters the *Forest of Persuasion* and *On Difficulties*. Each of these men spoke out because he could not help himself—there was no lack of instigation. Mencius, likewise, sought to stop hypocrites in order to bring back the constant norms, and Master Ouyang Xiu, by rebutting the Buddhists, restored the fundamentals.[13] Although their efforts to save the world differed in each case, the solutions are the same in their essentials.

This collection does more than correct minor deficiencies: it exposes the seedlings of falsehood in this age of decadence and uproots every last shoot; it lays bare the fiendish motivations of the treacherous and their closely guarded secrets. The elder head of household can use it to guide his sons and grandsons away from the clutches of evildoers. The young man on the road who follows its teachings can ward off villains and avoid the traps of experienced crooks. Let them try their thousands of tricks—their cleverness will not exceed what is found in this collection. It carries the title *Strange Tales from the Rivers and Lakes* because it records the vices of this late age. It is also known as *A New Book for Foiling Swindlers* because it reveals methods for salvation. Its prodigious contributions will endure far into the future; these few words of mine merely summarize its content.

Written on an auspicious day in the first month of the *dingsi* year of the Wanli period [1617] by Xiong Zhenji, Hermit of the Three Peaks.

Notes

1. Lu Ban 魯班 (trad. fifth century B.C.E.) was famed as an engineer, master craftsman, and inventor, notably of siege weapons; his contemporary the philosopher Mo Di 墨翟 was expert in defensive warfare. The whole preface is dense with classical allusions, which we have annotated only where further information is necessary to understand the text. It does not appear in any Ming imprint that we have seen, but is preserved in a handwritten copy in the National Archives of Japan (see bibliography for details). For an annotated version and Japanese translation see Itō Kanako, et al., "*Tohen shinsho" yakuchū kō shohen*, 2015, 121–29.

2. Because of its extreme hardness, jade cannot be cut with ordinary tools; instead it was worked with an abrasive (typically wet sand). The basin of water presumably reflects candlelight onto the face of a person using a mirror for their toilette. In both cases, as elsewhere in this passage, the author gives examples of how one might use humble or indirect means to achieve a more lofty objective. His suggestion seems to be that countering swindles and knavery calls for similar resourcefulness.

3. The latter alludes to a stratagem employed by the Han military leader Chen Ping 陳平 (d. 178 B.C.E.), who lifted a Xiongnu siege by using mannequins to create a false show of strength.

4. Zhuangzi records a story in which such a balm was crucial to a military victory. *Zhuangzi jijie* 莊子集解, ed. Wang Xianqian 王先謙 (Beijing: Zhonghua shuju, 1987), 7.

5. In a story recorded by the Warring States thinker Han Fei, thorn carving is a frivolous and perhaps impossible skill: an artisan who boasts that he can sculpt a tiny simian from a thorn is kept on as a court retainer but flees when called upon to demonstrate his art. *Han Fei zi jishi* 韓非子集釋, ed. Chen Qiyou 陳奇猷 (Beijing: Zhonghua shuju, 1958), 626–27.

6. "Precious raft," *baofa* 寶筏, is a Buddhist term for the dharma that ferries souls to salvation.

7. On these *yu* 蜮, a kind of water demon, see Carla Nappi, *The Monkey and the Inkpot: Natural History and Its Transformations in Early Modern China* (Cambridge, Mass.: Harvard University Press, 2009), 101–5.

8. In the first of these well-known parables, a treacherous eunuch offers a deer to the Second Emperor of the Qin (r. 210–207 B.C.E.), insisting that it is in fact a horse; he then identifies as allies and enemies respectively those who acquiesce to or reject his patently false description. (The Qin dynasty collapsed later that year.) In the second, a fox about to be devoured by a tiger saves itself by claiming to be the most fearsome of all beasts; it asks the tiger to follow and watch as all creatures flee before it. The tiger is

convinced, not realizing that itself, not the fox, is the one scaring the other animals.

9. This alludes to a story told in the early medieval text *Liezi* about a trainer who tricks his intelligent simian charges by redistributing, rather than increasing, their feedings. *Liezi jishi* 列子集釋, ed. Yang Bojun 楊伯峻 (Beijing: Zhonghua shuju, 1979), 86.

10. According to his biography in the *Jin shu* 晉書, the official Wei Jiao 溫嶠 (288–329) revealed a hidden aquatic creature near Ox Islet by burning a rhino horn; Ji Huanzi 季桓子 is an unrelated figure who discovered a strange animal in a well. The author may have conflated these two stories because they appear in close proximity in a famous tenth-century encyclopedia, the *Imperial Conspectus of the Taiping Era*. See Li Fang 李昉 (925–996), et al., *Taiping yulan* 太平御覽 (Beijing: Zhonghua shuju, 1963), *juan* 885. Cf. Fang Xuanling 房玄齡, ed., *Jin shu* (Beijing: Zhonghua shuju, 1974), 67.1795–96. The Qin palace, according to legend, had full-length mirrors whose reflections, like medical scans, revealed the viscera of the person imaged. The illustrations that start each of the four *juan* of the Ming woodblock edition of the *Book of Swindles* are based on allusions in this paragraph.

11. Jutan refers to a site in Jianyang, Fujian, where an academy was constructed in the Song period (960–1279). This attributed place of origin contradicts the chapter headings of the book, which identify Zhang as a native of Zhejiang province. There are several possible explanations. Xiong shows no evidence here that he knew anything about Zhang beyond what he could have gleaned from a draft, or even a mere description, of the book, so he might have mistakenly assumed that since Zhang contacted him from Jianyang he was also a native of that area. It is equally possible that although Zhang lived and was even born in Jianyang, his family had migrated there from Zhejiang and retained its nominal registration in Zhejiang. It is even conceivable that the publisher imagined that labeling the author Zhejiangese would increase the appeal of his work.

12. Yu 禹 was a legendary sage-ruler of early antiquity and the founder of the Xia dynasty; he is said to have cast a set of nine vessels with encyclopedic representations of creation that later became insignia of legitimate rule. To the Divine Farmer, Shennong 神農, is attributed an early pharmacopoeia recording the nutritional and therapeutic properties of *materia medica*, especially botanicals. The Duke of Zhou, regent for the third Zhou king in the eleventh century B.C.E., is the reputed author of part of the *Book of Changes*.

13. Both the Warring States philosopher Mencius (372–289 B.C.E.) and the Song period thinker Ouyang Xiu 歐陽修 (1007–1072) critiqued what they saw as the heterodox teachings of their times.

Appendix 2

Story Finding List

The table that follows lists all the stories in *Dupian xinshu* in their original order. It indicates, under the heading CRT, the *juan* and pages where the story can be located in our base text (the copy of the Cunren tang edition held in the library of the Tōyō Bunka Kenkyūjo of the University of Tokyo). For example, "Handing Over Silver Before Running Off with It" can be found on pages 4a (first side of the leaf numbered 4) to 5b (second side of the leaf numbered 5) in *juan* 1. The rightmost column, BoS, gives page numbers for the stories translated in this book.

Note that there are discrepancies between the titles of stories as they appear in the table of contents and the main text of the Cunren tang edition. We have generally relied on the title appearing in the text but have corrected obvious errors.

Type	Chinese Title	English Title	CRT	BoS
脫剝騙 Misdirection and Theft	假馬脫緞	Stealing Silk with a Decoy Horse	1.1a–4a	2–5
	先寄銀而後招逃	Handing Over Silver Before Running Off with It	1.4a–5b	6–8
	明騙販豬	A Clever Trick on a Pig Seller	1.5a–7a	9–10
	遇里長及脫茶壺	Encountering the Village Head and Then Stealing a Teapot	1.7a–9a	10–13
	乘鬧明竊店中布	Taking Advantage of the Bustle in a Shop to Brazenly Steal a Bolt of Cloth	1.9a–10a	
	詐稱偷鵝脫菁布	Pilfering Green Cloth by Pretending to Steal a Goose	1.10b–12a	
	借他人屋以脫布	Borrowing a Storefront to Steal Cloth	1.12a–14a	
	詐匠修換錢桌廚	A Fake Carpenter Fixes a Money Changer's Desk Drawer	1.14a–15a	
丟包騙 The Bag Drop	路途丟包行脫換	Dropping a Bag by the Roadside to Set Up a Switcheroo	1.15a–16b	15–17
換銀騙 Money Changing	成錠假銀換真銀	Swapping Fake Silver for a Pure Ingot	1.16b–18a	
	道士船中換真金	A Daoist in a Boat Exchanges Some Gold	1.18a–20a	19–22
詐哄騙 Misrepresentation	詐學道書報好夢	Forged Letters from the Education Intendant Report Auspicious Dreams	1.20a–22a	24–27
	詐無常燒騙捕人	Gulling People by Impersonating an Envoy from the Netherworld and Burning a Register	1.22a–24a	

(continued)

Type	Chinese Title	English Title	CRT	BoS
謀財騙 Scheming for Wealth	盜商伏財反喪財	Stealing a Business Partner's Riches Only to Lose One's Own	2.5b–8b	60–64
	傲氣致訟傷財命	Haughtiness Leads to a Lawsuit That Harms Wealth and Health	2.7a–12b	65–70
	輪抬童生人醉路	Sedan Bearers Take a Confucian Apprentice Off the Beaten Path	2.12b–14a	
	高抬重價反失利	Jacking Up the Price of Goods Only to End Up Ruined	2.14a–15b	
盜劫騙 Robbery	公子租屋劫寡婦	A Fake Scion Rents Rooms and Robs a Widow	2.15b–17b	
	詐脫貨物劫當鋪	Robbing a Pawnshop by Pretending to Leave Goods There	2.17b–19a	72–74
	京城店中響馬賊	A Highwayman Robs a Shop in the Capital	2.19a–20b	
強搶騙 Violence	私打印記占鋪陳	Acquiring a Bedroll by Marking It in Secret	2.20b–22a	
	賣藥貼眼搶元寶	Sticking a Plaster in the Eyes to Steal a Silver Ingot	2.22a–23a	76–77
	石灰撒眼以搶銀	Stealing Silver by Throwing Lime in the Eyes	2.23a–23b	
	大解被棍白日搶	Robbed by Crooks in Broad Daylight While Taking a Dump	2.23b–24a	
在船騙 On Boats	船載家人行李逃	Luggage Aboard a Boat Disappears, Along with a Family Member	2.24a–25b	
	娶妾在船夜被拐	A New Concubine Is Kidnapped from a Boat at Night	2.25b–27b	
	買銅物被艄謀死	A Purchase of Copperware Incites Boatmen to Murder	2.27b–30b	

(continued)

[1]Includes four additional stories.
[2]Includes one additional story.

Bibliography

Early Copies of *Dupian xinshu*

Dingke Jianghu lilan dupian xinshu 鼎刻江湖歷覽杜騙新書. Late-Ming woodblock edition, Cunren tang, Jianyang, Fujian. Tōyō Bunka Kenkyūjo (Institute for Advanced Studies on Asia) of the University of Tokyo, formerly in the Sōkōdō 雙紅堂. A woodblock illustration appears at the head of each of four *juan*. Some leaves replaced with handwritten copies in a Japanese hand. Photoreproduction at http://shanben.ioc.u-tokyo.ac.jp/main_p.php?nu=D8624000&order=rn_no&no=04481 (accessed November 13, 2016).

Dingke Jianghu lilan dupian xinshu 鼎刻江湖歷覽杜騙新書. Late-Ming woodblock edition, Cunren tang, Jianyang, Fujian. A woodblock illustration appears at the head of each of four *juan*. Harvard-Yenching Library. Leaf 1.47 missing. Photoreproduction at http://nrs.harvard.edu/urn-3:FHCL:26866101 (accessed November 13, 2016).

Dingke Jianghu lilan dupian xinshu 鼎刻江湖歷覽杜騙新書. Early Edo period manuscript copy of Ming woodblock edition of Juren tang, Fujian, Jianyang. Includes 1617 Xiong Zhenji preface; no illustrations. Owned, and likely annotated, by Hayashi Razan 林羅山 (1583–1657). National Archives of Japan, Call No. 300–054, formerly in the Cabinet Library. Photoreproduction at http://www.digital.archives.go.jp/das/image/F1000000000000102866 (accessed November 13, 2016).

Dingke Jianghu lilan dupian xinshu 鼎刻江湖歷覽杜騙新書. Wanli-period woodblock edition. National Archives of Japan, formerly in the Cabinet Library. Call No. 300–059. Not seen.

Dingke Jianghu lilan dupian xinshu 鼎刻江湖歷覽杜騙新書. Wanli-period woodblock edition. Sonkeikaku 尊経閣, Tokyo. Not seen.

Selected Modern Editions of *Dupian xinshu*, in Chronological Order

Dupian xinshu 杜騙新書. In *Ming-Qing shanben xiaoshuo congkan chubian* 明清善本小說叢刊初編, Series 3. Taipei: Tianyi chubanshe, [1985?]. Photoreproduction of copy at Harvard-Yenching Library.

Dupian xinshu 杜騙新書. In *Guben xiaoshuo jicheng* 古本小說集成, Series 3. Shanghai: Shanghai guji chubanshe, [1990?]. Photoreproduction of copy at Harvard-Yenching Library.

Dupian xinshu 杜騙新書. In *Guben xiaoshuo congkan* 古本小說叢刊, Series 35, Vol. 3. Beijing: Zhonghua shuju, 1991. Photoreproduction of copy at Harvard-Yenching Library.

Jianghu qiwen dupian xinshu 江湖奇聞杜騙新書. Ed. Meng Zhaolian 孟昭連. Tianjin: Baihua wenyi chubanshe, 1992.

Jianghu lilan dupian xinshu 江湖曆覽杜騙新書. Beijing: Tuanjie chubanshe, 1993.

Fangpian midian 防騙秘典. Ed. Kang Huiyi 康暉宜. Guangzhou: Guangzhou chubanshe, 1993.

Jianghu qiwen dupian xinshu 江湖奇聞杜騙新書. Ed. Liao Dong 廖東. Zhengzhou: Zhongzhou guji chubanshe, 1994.

Dupian xinshu 杜騙新書. In *Zhongguo gudai zhenxiben xiaoshuo* 中國古代珍稀本小說. Shenyang: Chunfeng wenyi chubanshe, 1994.

Xinke jianghu dupian shu: Zhongguo gudai diyi bu fan zhapian qishu 新刻江湖杜騙術: 中國古代第一部反詐騙奇書. Ed. Ji Fan 紀凡. Shijiazhuang: Hebei jiaoyu chubanshe, 1995.

Fangpian jing: Jianghu qiwen dupian xinshu *jinyi jinjie* 防騙經：《江湖奇聞—杜騙新書》今譯今解. Ed. Ding Xiaoshan 丁曉山. Beijing: Zhongguo wenlian chuban gongsi, 1997.

Pian jing 騙經. In *Zhongguo jinhui xiaoshuo baibu* 中國禁毀小說百部. Beijing: Dazhong wenhua chubanshe, 1999.

Pian jing 騙經. Guilin: Guangxi shifan daxue chubanshe, 2008.

Other Sources Cited

Alpert, Michael, trans. *Lazarillo de Tormes and The Swindler: Two Spanish Picaresque Novels*. Rev. ed. New York: Penguin, 2003.

Altenburger, Roland. "Täuschung und Prävention: Ambiguitäten einer Sammlung von Fallgeschichten aus der späten Ming-Zeit." In *Harmonie und Konflikt in China*, ed. Christian Soffel and Tilman Schalmey, 109–27. Jahrbuch der Deutschen Vereinigung für China-Studien, 9. Wiesbaden: Harrassowitz Verlag, 2014.

Brook, Timothy. *The Confusions of Pleasure: Commerce and Culture in Ming China*. Berkeley: University of California Press, 1999.

Chia, Lucille. *Printing for Profit: The Commercial Publishers of Jianyang, Fujian (11th–17th Centuries)*. Cambridge, MA: Harvard University Asia Center, 2003.

Fang Xuanling 房玄齡, ed. *Jin shu* 晉書. Beijing: Zhonghua shuju, 1974.

Gao Qi 高啓. *Daquan ji* 大全集. In *Wenyuan ge Siku quanshu* 文淵閣四庫全書. Photoreproduction of late-Qing manuscript copy. Taipei: Shangwu yinshuguan, 1983.

Han Dacheng 韓大成. *Mingdai chengshi yanjiu* 明代城市研究. Beijing: Zhongguo renmin daxue chubanshe, 1991.

Han Fei zi jishi 韓非子集釋. Ed. Chen Qiyou 陳奇猷. Beijing: Zhonghua shuju, 1958.

Hanan, Patrick. "The Making of *The Pearl-Sewn Shirt* and *The Courtesan's Jewel Box*." *Harvard Journal of Asiatic Studies* 33, no. 3–4 (1973): 124–53.

He, Yuming. *Home and the World: Editing the "Glorious Ming" in Woodblock-Printed Books of the Sixteenth and Seventeenth Centuries*. Cambridge, MA: Harvard University Asia Center, 2013.

Itō Kanako 伊藤加奈子, et al. *"Tohen shinsho" yakuchū kō shohen*「杜騙新書」訳注稿初編. N.p.: "Tohen Shinsho" no Kisoteki Kenkyū Purojekuto, 2015.

Lai, T. C. *T'ang Yin, Poet/painter, 1470–1524*. Hong Kong: Kelly and Walsh, 1971.

Lei Junyao 雷君曜, ed. *Huitu pianshu qitan* 繪圖騙術奇談. 4 vols. Shanghai: Saoye shanfang, 1909.

Lenz, William E. *Fast Talk and Flush Times: The Confidence Man as a Literary Convention*. Columbia: University of Missouri Press, 1985.

Li Fang 李昉, et al. *Taiping guangji* 太平廣記. Beijing: Zhonghua shuju, 1961.

——. *Taiping yulan* 太平御覽. Beijing: Zhonghua shuju, 1963.

Li Sha 李莎. "'Da qiufeng' yuyuan kaoshi'" 打秋風"語源考釋. *Guangxi minzu xueyuan xuebao (zhexue shehui kexue ban)* 廣西民族學院學報 (哲學社會科學版) S2 (December 2001): 239–40.

Liezi jishi 列子集釋. Ed. Yang Bojun 楊伯峻. Beijing: Zhonghua shuju, 1979.

Lu, Tina. *Accidental Incest, Filial Cannibalism, and Other Peculiar Encounters in Late Imperial Chinese Literature*. Cambridge, MA: Harvard University Asia Center, 2008.

Maurer, David. *The Big Con: The Story of the Confidence Man*. New York: Anchor, 1999 [1940].

McNicholas, Mark. *Forgery and Impersonation in Imperial China: Popular Deceptions and the High Qing State*. Seattle: University of Washington Press, 2016.

Nappi, Carla. *The Monkey and the Inkpot: Natural History and Its Transformations in Early Modern China*. Cambridge, MA: Harvard University Press, 2009.

Niu Jianqiang 牛建強. "Wan Ming duanpian shiqing xiaoshuoji *Dupian xinshu* banbenkao" 晚明短篇世情小說集《杜騙新書》版本考. *Wenxian jikan* 文獻季刊 3 (July 2000): 200–10.

Rolston, David L. *Traditional Chinese Fiction and Fiction Commentary: Reading and Writing Between the Lines*. Stanford: Stanford University Press, 1997.

Sima Qian 司馬遷. *Shiji* 史記. Beijing: Zhonghua shuju, 1982.

Slingerland, Edward G. *Confucius Analects: With Selection from Traditional Commentaries*. Indianapolis: Hackett, 2003.

Song Yingxing 宋應星. *Tiangong kaiwu* 天工開物. 1637 woodblock ed.

Tang Yin 唐寅. *Tang Bohu shi jiyi jianzhu* 唐伯虎詩輯逸箋注. Ed. Zheng Qian 鄭騫. Taipei: Lianjing, 1982.

——. *Tang Bohu xiansheng quanji* 唐伯虎先生全集. 2 vols. Photoreproduction of 1614 Nanya tang ed. Taipei: Xuesheng shuju, 1970.

Wu Zhaoyang 吳朝陽. "*Dupian xinshu* Fujian difang shuxing kaoshu" 《杜騙新書》福建地方屬性考述, *Ming-Qing xiaoshuo yanjiu* 明清小說研究 113, no. 3 (2014): 161–72.

Xin Yu 辛羽. "'Da qiufeng' xiaokao" "打秋風"小考. *Yaowen juezi* 咬文嚼字 7 (2012): 40–42.

Youd, Daniel M. "Beyond *Bao*: Moral Ambiguity and the Law in Late Imperial Chinese Narrative Literature." In *Writing and Law in Late Imperial China: Crime, Conflict, and Judgment*, ed. Robert E. Hegel and Katherine Carlitz, 215–33. Seattle: University of Washington Press, 2007.

Zhou Hui 周暉. *Jinling suoshi* 金陵瑣事. 2 vols. Beijing: Wenxue guji kanxingshe, 1955.

Zhuangzi jijie 莊子集解. Ed. Wang Xianqian 王先謙. Beijing: Zhonghua shuju, 1987.

TRANSLATIONS FROM THE ASIAN CLASSICS

Major Plays of Chikamatsu, tr. Donald Keene 1961

Four Major Plays of Chikamatsu, tr. Donald Keene. Paperback ed. only. 1961; rev. ed. 1997

Records of the Grand Historian of China, translated from the Shih chi of Ssu-ma Ch'ien, tr. Burton Watson, 2 vols. 1961

Instructions for Practical Living and Other Neo-Confucian Writings by Wang Yang-ming, tr. Wing-tsit Chan 1963

Hsün Tzu: Basic Writings, tr. Burton Watson, paperback ed. only. 1963; rev. ed. 1996

Chuang Tzu: Basic Writings, tr. Burton Watson, paperback ed. only. 1964; rev. ed. 1996

The Mahābhārata, tr. Chakravarthi V. Narasimhan. Also in paperback ed. 1965; rev. ed. 1997

The Manyōshū, Nippon Gakujutsu Shinkōkai edition 1965

Su Tung-p'o: Selections from a Sung Dynasty Poet, tr. Burton Watson. Also in paperback ed. 1965

Bhartrihari: Poems, tr. Barbara Stoler Miller. Also in paperback ed. 1967

Basic Writings of Mo Tzu, Hsün Tzu, and Han Fei Tzu, tr. Burton Watson. Also in separate paperback eds. 1967

The Awakening of Faith, Attributed to Aśvaghosha, tr. Yoshito S. Hakeda. Also in paperback ed. 1967

Reflections on Things at Hand: The Neo-Confucian Anthology, comp. Chu Hsi and Lü Tsu-ch'ien, tr. Wing-tsit Chan 1967

The Platform Sutra of the Sixth Patriarch, tr. Philip B. Yampolsky. Also in paperback ed. 1967

Essays in Idleness: The Tsurezuregusa of Kenkō, tr. Donald Keene. Also in paperback ed. 1967

The Pillow Book of Sei Shōnagon, tr. Ivan Morris, 2 vols. 1967

Two Plays of Ancient India: The Little Clay Cart and the Minister's Seal, tr. J. A. B. van Buitenen 1968

The Complete Works of Chuang Tzu, tr. Burton Watson 1968

The Romance of the Western Chamber (Hsi Hsiang chi), tr. S. I. Hsiung. Also in paperback ed. 1968

The Manyōshū, Nippon Gakujutsu Shinkōkai edition. Paperback ed. only. 1969

Records of the Historian: Chapters from the Shih chi of Ssu-ma Ch'ien, tr. Burton Watson. Paperback ed. only. 1969

Cold Mountain: 100 Poems by the T'ang Poet Han-shan, tr. Burton Watson. Also in paperback ed. 1970

Twenty Plays of the Nō Theatre, ed. Donald Keene. Also in paperback ed. 1970

Chūshingura: The Treasury of Loyal Retainers, tr. Donald Keene. Also in paperback ed. 1971; rev. ed. 1997

The Zen Master Hakuin: Selected Writings, tr. Philip B. Yampolsky 1971

Chinese Rhyme-Prose: Poems in the Fu Form from the Han and Six Dynasties Periods, tr. Burton Watson. Also in paperback ed. 1971

Kūkai: Major Works, tr. Yoshito S. Hakeda. Also in paperback ed. 1972

The Old Man Who Does as He Pleases: Selections from the Poetry and Prose of Lu Yu, tr. Burton Watson 1973

The Lion's Roar of Queen Śrīmālā, tr. Alex and Hideko Wayman 1974

Courtier and Commoner in Ancient China: Selections from the History of the Former Han by Pan Ku, tr. Burton Watson. Also in paperback ed. 1974

Japanese Literature in Chinese, vol. 1: *Poetry and Prose in Chinese by Japanese Writers of the Early Period*, tr. Burton Watson 1975

Japanese Literature in Chinese, vol. 2: *Poetry and Prose in Chinese by Japanese Writers of the Later Period*, tr. Burton Watson 1976

Love Song of the Dark Lord: Jayadeva's Gītagovinda, tr. Barbara Stoler Miller. Also in paperback ed. Cloth ed. includes critical text of the Sanskrit. 1977; rev. ed. 1997

Ryōkan: Zen Monk-Poet of Japan, tr. Burton Watson 1977

Calming the Mind and Discerning the Real: From the Lam rim chen mo of Tsoṇ-kha-pa, tr. Alex Wayman 1978

The Hermit and the Love-Thief: Sanskrit Poems of Bhartrihari and Bilhaṇa, tr. Barbara Stoler Miller 1978

The Lute: Kao Ming's P'i-p'a chi, tr. Jean Mulligan. Also in paperback ed. 1980

A Chronicle of Gods and Sovereigns: Jinnō Shōtōki of Kitabatake Chikafusa, tr. H. Paul Varley 1980

Among the Flowers: The Hua-chien chi, tr. Lois Fusek 1982

Grass Hill: Poems and Prose by the Japanese Monk Gensei, tr. Burton Watson 1983

Doctors, Diviners, and Magicians of Ancient China: Biographies of Fang-shih, tr. Kenneth J. DeWoskin. Also in paperback ed. 1983

Theater of Memory: The Plays of Kālidāsa, ed. Barbara Stoler Miller. Also in paperback ed. 1984

The Columbia Book of Chinese Poetry: From Early Times to the Thirteenth Century, ed. and tr. Burton Watson. Also in paperback ed. 1984

Poems of Love and War: From the Eight Anthologies and the Ten Long Poems of Classical Tamil, tr. A. K. Ramanujan. Also in paperback ed. 1985

The Bhagavad Gita: Krishna's Counsel in Time of War, tr. Barbara Stoler Miller 1986

The Columbia Book of Later Chinese Poetry, ed. and tr. Jonathan Chaves. Also in paperback
ed. 1986

The Tso Chuan: Selections from China's Oldest Narrative History, tr. Burton Watson 1989

Waiting for the Wind: Thirty-six Poets of Japan's Late Medieval Age, tr. Steven Carter 1989

Selected Writings of Nichiren, ed. Philip B. Yampolsky 1990

Saigyō, Poems of a Mountain Home, tr. Burton Watson 1990

The Book of Lieh Tzu: A Classic of the Tao, tr. A. C. Graham. Morningside ed. 1990

The Tale of an Anklet: An Epic of South India—The Cilappatikāram of Iḷaṅkō Aṭikaḷ, tr.
R. Parthasarathy 1993

Waiting for the Dawn: A Plan for the Prince, tr. with introduction by Wm. Theodore de
Bary 1993

*Yoshitsune and the Thousand Cherry Trees: A Masterpiece of the Eighteenth-Century Japanese
Puppet Theater*, tr., annotated, and with introduction by Stanleigh H. Jones Jr. 1993

The Lotus Sutra, tr. Burton Watson. Also in paperback ed. 1993

The Classic of Changes: A New Translation of the I Ching as Interpreted by Wang Bi, tr.
Richard John Lynn 1994

Beyond Spring: Tz'u Poems of the Sung Dynasty, tr. Julie Landau 1994

The Columbia Anthology of Traditional Chinese Literature, ed. Victor H. Mair 1994

Scenes for Mandarins: The Elite Theater of the Ming, tr. Cyril Birch 1995

Letters of Nichiren, ed. Philip B. Yampolsky; tr. Burton Watson et al. 1996

Unforgotten Dreams: Poems by the Zen Monk Shōtetsu, tr. Steven D. Carter 1997

The Vimalakirti Sutra, tr. Burton Watson 1997

Japanese and Chinese Poems to Sing: The Wakan rōei shū, tr. J. Thomas Rimer and
Jonathan Chaves 1997

Breeze Through Bamboo: Kanshi of Ema Saikō, tr. Hiroaki Sato 1998

A Tower for the Summer Heat, by Li Yu, tr. Patrick Hanan 1998

Traditional Japanese Theater: An Anthology of Plays, by Karen Brazell 1998

*The Original Analects: Sayings of Confucius and His Successors
(0479–0249)*, by E. Bruce Brooks and A. Taeko Brooks 1998

*The Classic of the Way and Virtue: A New Translation of the Tao-te ching of Laozi as
Interpreted by Wang Bi*, tr. Richard John Lynn 1999

*The Four Hundred Songs of War and Wisdom: An Anthology of Poems from Classical Tamil,
The Puṟanāṉūṟu*, ed. and tr. George L. Hart
and Hank Heifetz 1999

Original Tao: Inward Training (Nei-yeh) *and the Foundations of Taoist Mysticism*, by
Harold D. Roth 1999

Po Chü-i: Selected Poems, tr. Burton Watson 2000

Lao Tzu's Tao Te Ching: A Translation of the Startling New Documents Found at Guodian,
by Robert G. Henricks 2000

The Shorter Columbia Anthology of Traditional Chinese Literature, ed. Victor H. Mair 2000

Mistress and Maid (Jiaohongji), by Meng Chengshun, tr. Cyril Birch 2001

Chikamatsu: Five Late Plays, tr. and ed. C. Andrew Gerstle 2001

The Essential Lotus: Selections from the Lotus Sutra, tr. Burton Watson 2002

Early Modern Japanese Literature: An Anthology, 1600–1900, ed. Haruo Shirane 2002;
abridged 2008

The Columbia Anthology of Traditional Korean Poetry, ed. Peter H. Lee 2002

The Sound of the Kiss, or The Story That Must Never Be Told: Pingali Suranna's Kalapurno-
dayamu, tr. Vecheru Narayana Rao and David Shulman 2003

The Selected Poems of Du Fu, tr. Burton Watson 2003

Far Beyond the Field: Haiku by Japanese Women, tr. Makoto Ueda 2003

Just Living: Poems and Prose by the Japanese Monk Tonna, ed. and tr. Steven D. Carter 2003

Han Feizi: Basic Writings, tr. Burton Watson 2003

Mozi: Basic Writings, tr. Burton Watson 2003

Xunzi: Basic Writings, tr. Burton Watson 2003

Zhuangzi: Basic Writings, tr. Burton Watson 2003

The Awakening of Faith, Attributed to Aśvaghosha, tr. Yoshito S. Hakeda, introduction by
Ryuichi Abe 2005

The Tales of the Heike, tr. Burton Watson, ed. Haruo Shirane 2006

Tales of Moonlight and Rain, by Ueda Akinari, tr. with introduction by Anthony H.
Chambers 2007

Traditional Japanese Literature: An Anthology, Beginnings to 1600, ed. Haruo Shirane 2007

The Philosophy of Qi, by Kaibara Ekken, tr. Mary Evelyn Tucker 2007

The Analects of Confucius, tr. Burton Watson 2007

The Art of War: Sun Zi's Military Methods, tr. Victor Mair 2007

One Hundred Poets, One Poem Each: A Translation of the Ogura Hyakunin Isshu, tr. Peter
McMillan 2008

Zeami: Performance Notes, tr. Tom Hare 2008

Zongmi on Chan, tr. Jeffrey Lyle Broughton 2009

Scripture of the Lotus Blossom of the Fine Dharma, rev. ed., tr. Leon Hurvitz, preface and
introduction by Stephen R. Teiser 2009

Mencius, tr. Irene Bloom, ed. with an introduction by Philip J. Ivanhoe 2009

Clouds Thick, Whereabouts Unknown: Poems by Zen Monks of China, Charles Egan 2010

The Mozi: A Complete Translation, tr. Ian Johnston 2010

The Huainanzi: A Guide to the Theory and Practice of Government in Early Han China, by
Liu An, tr. and ed. John S. Major, Sarah A. Queen, Andrew Seth Meyer, and Harold
D. Roth, with Michael Puett and Judson Murray 2010

The Demon at Agi Bridge and Other Japanese Tales, tr. Burton Watson, ed. with
introduction by Haruo Shirane 2011

Haiku Before Haiku: From the Renga Masters to Bashō, tr. with introduction by Steven D.
Carter 2011

The Columbia Anthology of Chinese Folk and Popular Literature, ed. Victor H. Mair and
Mark Bender 2011

Milton Keynes UK
Ingram Content Group UK Ltd.
UKHW011950290923
429652UK00005B/262